THE FRANCIS PROJECT

The Francis Project

Where He Wants
to Take the Church

Víctor Manuel Fernández
in Conversation with Paolo Rodari

Paulist Press
New York / Mahwah, NJ

Originally published by EMI, Via di Corticella, 179/4 – 40128 Bologna, Italy, as *Il progetto di Francesco: Dove vuole portare la Chiesa* by Víctor Manuel Fernández in dialogue with Paolo Rodari, © EMI, 2014.

Cover image: CNS photo/Paul Haring
Cover design by Phyllis Campos
Book design by Lynn Else

Library of Congress Cataloging-in-Publication Data

Names: Fernández, Víctor M. (Víctor Manuel), 1962– author. | Rodari, Paolo.
Title: The Francis project : where he wants to take the church / Víctor Manuel
    Fernández in conversation with Paolo Rodari.
Other titles: Il progetto di Francesco. English
Description: New York : Paulist Press, 2016.
Identifiers: LCCN 2015038518 (print) | LCCN 2016001182 (ebook) | ISBN
    9780809149636 (pbk. : alk. paper) | ISBN 9781587685750 (ebook) | ISBN
    9781587685750 (Ebook)
Subjects: LCSH: Francis, Pope, 1936– | Catholic Church. Pope (2013- : Francis)
    Evangelii gaudium. | Church. | Evangelistic work—Catholic Church. | Catholic
    Church—Doctrines.
Classification: LCC BX1378.7 .F473 2016 (print) | LCC BX1378.7 (ebook) | DDC
    282.092—dc23
LC record available at http://lccn.loc.gov/2015038518

ISBN 978-0-8091-4963-6 (paperback)
ISBN 978-1-58768-575-0 (e-book)

Published by Paulist Press
997 Macarthur Boulevard
Mahwah, New Jersey 07430

www.paulistpress.com

Printed and bound in the
United States of America

*Those who take most advantage of life's possibilities
are those who leave the safety of the shore
and are passionate about the mission
of communicating life to others.*

Aparecida Document, 360

Contents

Abbreviations

AD – *Aparecida Document* (Concluding Document of the Fifth General Conference of the Latin American and Caribbean Bishops). The General Council of the Bishops of Latin America and the Carribean (Aparecida, Brazil, May 13–31, 2007).

EG – *Evangelii Gaudium* (Apostolic Exhortation of Pope Francis on the Proclamation of the Gospel in Today's World). Pope Francis, November 24, 2013. http://w2.vatican.va/content/francesco/en/apost_exhortations/documents/papa-francesco_esortazione-ap_20131124_evangelii-gaudium.html.

RM – *Redemptoris Missio* (Encyclical Letter on the Permanent Validity of the Church's Missionary Mandate). Pope John Paul II, December 7, 1990.

UR – *Unitatis Redintegratio* (Decree of the Second Vatican Council on Ecumenism). Holy See, November 21, 1964.

UUS – *Ut Unum Sint* (Encyclical Letter on the Commitment to Ecumenism). Pope John Paul II, May 25, 1995.

Introduction

The Purpose of
Evangelii Gaudium

Paolo Rodari

March 13, 2013. Where does Francis want to take the Church? This is the question I asked myself during the first days of Jorge Mario Bergoglio's pontificate. And, as a reporter, since I had a responsibility to report on the pontificate in progress, I have asked this same question of everyone I have met or listened to in the course of my work ever since the conclave ended. "You know that the duty of the conclave was to provide a bishop for Rome, and it seems that my brother cardinals have gone to the ends of the earth to find one…but here we are," Pope Francis said as he looked out from the central loggia of the Vatican Basilica on the evening of his election. What does it mean, I asked myself, to have a pope who is from "the ends of the earth"? What will he bring to the Church? And most importantly, where will he take it?

A few days after the election, I called a bishop friend. I was planning to carry out a survey among the Jesuits and asked him his opinion about what questions to ask and, in particular, what to ask about the new pope. He replied,

Have you read *On Heaven and Earth*, the book that Bergoglio wrote with Rabbi Abraham Skórka? For me, the most illuminating chapters were those in which both of them confront the so-called ethically sensitive issues: marriage between a man and a woman, abortion, euthanasia, etc. Reading them, I seem to have understood that for Bergoglio what comes before the principles and their defense is the kerygma, or the announcement of the good news of the gospel. It seems to me that this is the main thrust of the new pope: the principles do exist and no one denies that, but first we must announce that the gospel is love, mercy, an embrace. It is useless to focus too strongly on principles and it can be counterproductive.

September 19, 2013. It is morning. I am in Florence and the phone rings. They tell me that a long interview granted by the pope to Fr. Antonio Spadaro, director of *Civiltà Cattolica*, is just about to come out. I have the text sent to me. There are endless ideas, but more than anything else, I am struck by one particular part. The pope says, "We cannot focus only on issues related to abortion, gay marriage and the use of contraceptive methods. This is not possible. I have not spoken much about these things, and I was reprimanded for it. But when we speak about these things, we have to speak about them in a context. We know what the Church's opinion on these things is and I am the son of the Church, but it is not necessary to talk about them all the time." And again,

> The teachings, which are as much dogmatic as moral, are not all the same. A missionary ministry cannot be obsessed by transmitting a disjointed collection of doctrines to be imposed urgently. A missionary proclamation must concentrate on the essentials, on what is needed. This is also what fascinates and attracts

people more, what makes the heart burn as it did for the disciples at Emmaus. So we have to find a new balance, otherwise even the edifice of the Church's moral teaching risks becoming a house of cards and will cease to have the fragrance of the Gospel. What the Gospel has to offer should be simpler, deeper, and more radiant. It is from this proposition that the moral consequences then arise.

For me, these words are enlightening. They confirm that the first intuition that was suggested to me by my friend, the bishop, seems right: Francis appears to want a Church that embraces rather than excludes. And he believes that to insist too much, almost obsessively, on the principles is a tactic that is not in keeping with the gospel message. Of course, his predecessors also wanted a Church like this. But in Francis, this emphasis seems more pronounced.

October 21, 2013. My article is published in *La Repubblica*, detailing my interview with Víctor Manuel Fernández, rector of the Pontifical Catholic University of Argentina, one of Francis's first episcopal appointments, who was raised to the dignity of archbishop in May 2013. He is a gifted theologian and has a relationship of trust with the pope, who sees him as a valuable adviser.

It is no coincidence that in 2007, at the Fifth Conference of Latin American Bishops in Aparecida (São Paulo), it was Fernández who helped Bergoglio to draw up the final document that defined the future pope's idea of the Church. Therefore, there are few like Fernández who can help us understand who Francis is and where he wants the Church to end up. So, at the beginning of October, I called him in Buenos Aires. It was a friendly voice that answered. I explained my interest in the pope, my desire to understand him in depth and the characteristics of "his" Church. Fernández agreed to my sending him some questions, without guaranteeing a response. A few days later, however, he got in touch with me.

He did not avoid any questions, especially the issue that seemed most important to me, which was whether he believed that it could be said that Francis is the pope who values mercy over principles. He answered,

> The announcement of the heart of the Gospel before all else is an important feature of Francis's approach, but it should be understood in the context of a renewal of the Church's mission. The Pope thinks that a Church that wants to extend beyond its borders and reach everyone necessarily has to adapt its way of preaching. Above all, he applies the yardstick that was proposed by the Second Vatican Council but is often forgotten and overlooked: the "hierarchy of truths." Francis invites us to recognize that often the precepts of the moral teaching of the Church are presented without regard to the context that gives them meaning. The biggest problem is when the message that the Church proclaims is identified only with these aspects, which, however, do not show the heart of the message of Jesus Christ in its entirety.

And again,

> There must be a sense of proportion, especially in the frequency with which certain topics or emphases are placed in preaching. For example, if during the liturgical year a parish priest speaks about sexual morality ten times, and only two or three times of brotherly love or justice, then that is disproportionate. It is the same if he often speaks against gay marriage but not much about the beauty of marriage. Or if he speaks more about law than about grace, more about the Church than about Jesus Christ, or more about the pope than about the word of God.

Introduction

As a result of the *La Repubblica* interview, Fr. Fernández and I got to know each other better. This led me to make a further request: "Why don't we publish a book together on the subject of Francis, or rather on his 'plan'?" To my delight, Fr. Fernández agreed again. Together we decided to use the Apostolic Exhortation *Evangelii Gaudium* (EG) as a basis to work from, bearing in mind that it was the same pope who said that the document has a "programmatic" significance (EG 25). The time we spent together in Buenos Aires and the intense correspondence between us resulted in the book you have before you. It is a book that I hope will be useful for those who want to fully understand the challenge that the pope who came from "the ends of the earth" wants to lay before the Church, but also even for those who are far away from a life of faith.

Evangelii Gaudium is an extensive and precise plan for Francis's pontificate. In fact, this Apostolic Exhortation, which the pope signed on November 24, 2013, the Feast of Christ the King, formally should have been post-synodal or simply a development of the propositions produced by the Synod of Bishops held in the Vatican in 2012 and dedicated to the new evangelization. But, in fact, the document deliberately does not mention the term *post-synodal*, because it is, and wants to be, much more—an extensive planning document. We began with *Evangelii Gaudium*, and that made it easy for us to broaden the horizons of this surprising pope.

Evangelii Gaudium means "the joy of the Gospel" and this seems to be, first and foremost, its orientation: to bring the Church into an awareness that Christianity is joy because it announces that God is with us. One of the most popular actions emphasized by the pope is the need to "come out of ourselves": to come out from behind our beliefs, our comfort zones, our privileges, and our ideas, to bring the gospel of Christ to everyone without prejudice or exclusion. To emerge, to change, and therefore, to rethink our whole life of faith all over again. The pope does not shy away from pointing out specific reforms and changes, urging "everyone to apply the guidelines found in this document generously and courageously, without inhibitions or fear" (EG 33). This is no longer the time for bashfulness. Francis wants everyone, starting with the simple faithful, to abandon the convenient excuse of "we have always done it this way" (no. 33). He says, "I invite everyone to be bold and creative in this task of rethinking the goals, structures, style and methods of evangelization in their respective communities" (no. 33).

This book, therefore, is also a result of our amazement at this papal text, a true and proper encyclical, as many observers have written — amazement at a pope who decides to put in writing a plan that makes demands even of himself and his own person: "Since I am called to put into practice what I ask of others, I too must think about a conversion of the papacy" (EG 32). The work that Pope Francis has laid out in *Evangelii Gaudium* is broad enough to make you dizzy just reading it. "Yet," as Francis writes, "there is no greater freedom than that of allowing oneself to be guided by the Holy Spirit, renouncing the attempt to plan and control everything to the last detail, and instead letting him enlighten, guide, and direct us, leading us wherever he wills" (no. 280).

1

The Inspiration of
Francis of Assisi

On March 16, 2013, three days after his election to the See of Peter, during a meeting with journalists in the Paul VI Audience Hall at the Vatican, Jorge Mario Bergoglio revealed that many cardinals in the Sistine Chapel had tried to suggest to him which name he should choose. "One of them told me: 'You should call yourself Adrian, like the great reformer.' And, indeed, the Church must be reformed….Someone else said: 'You should call yourself Clement. Clement XV.' Why? 'Out of revenge for Clement XIV having abolished the Society of Jesus!'" But then, after speaking with Cardinal Claudio Hummes, who embraced him and asked him not to forget the poor, he decided to call himself Francis after the saint of poverty.

Who is St. Francis for the pope? Why did he want to take his name? The pope has spoken several times of St. Francis. And in speaking about him, he allows us to understand which of Francis's character traits are significant for him. But perhaps the most incisive and the clearest words he has spoken on the saint from Assisi were in the Umbrian town itself, during the pastoral visit that took place on October 4, 2013.

What shows us the life of St. Francis today? This is the question that the pope asked of the many faithful who came on pilgrimage with him. Bergoglio explained,

The first thing he tells us is that being a Christian is a vital relationship with the person of Jesus; it means putting on Jesus Christ, and being assimilated into Him. And where does St. Francis's journey toward Christ begin? It begins by looking at Jesus on the cross. In looking at him at the moment in which He gives his life for us and draws us to Himself. Francis had this experience especially in the little church of San Damiano, praying before the crucifix, which even today we can venerate. On that crucifix Jesus seems to be not dead, but alive! The blood streams from the wounds of his hands, feet and side, but that blood expresses life. Jesus does not have his eyes closed but open, wide open: a look that speaks to the heart. And the crucifix does not speak of defeat, of failure; paradoxically it speaks of a death that is life, and generates life, because it speaks of love, because it is the Love of God incarnate, and Love does not die, indeed, it conquers evil and death. Whoever allows himself to be looked upon by the crucified Jesus is recreated, becomes a "new creature." Everything begins with this: it is the experience of grace that transforms, being loved without having to earn it, even though we are sinners.

It is only by following him on the cross that we can have true life and be transformed in spite of sin. The poverty of St. Francis, therefore, is not primarily material. It is spiritual; it is of the heart: it means losing oneself in the cross of Jesus. Of course, divesting ourselves of worldly goods is necessary. And it helps. However, it is useless without opening our hearts to Jesus Christ.

The second thing that the saint taught the world is that, as the pope explained,

Those who follow Christ receive true peace, one that only he, and not the world, can give us. St. Francis is associated by many with peace, and this is right, but few go deeper. What is the peace that Francis accepted and lived and that is passed on to us? It is the peace of Christ, given to us through the greatest love, that of the Cross. It is the peace that the Risen Jesus gave to his disciples when he appeared in their midst: Franciscan peace is not a fuzzy feeling. That kind of St. Francis does not exist! Nor is it a kind of pantheistic harmony with the energies of the cosmos....This is not Franciscan either, but it is an idea that some have made up! The peace of St. Francis is that of Christ, and it can be found by "taking his yoke upon oneself," that is, his commandment: love one another as I have loved you. And you cannot bear this yoke with arrogance, with conceit, with pride; it can only be borne with meekness and humility of heart.

This is the second aspect of the personality of St. Francis: he was a man devoted to peace but not to pacifism without Christ. True peace enters our heart, the pope says, if we allow Jesus Christ, whose supreme commandment is charity, to enter. So it was in honor of this Francis that on March 13, 2013, Bergoglio chose his name: in honor of the saint who became like those who are last, the poor, not for love of poverty as an end in itself but because by following the poor and loving them, he was following and serving Christ crucified.

———————

Fr. Víctor, the "Church of the poor" usually refers to the movement that, since the Second Vatican Council, has prompted the thoughts and actions of the Catholic Church to rediscover a consistent commitment to solidarity with oppressed peoples and to formulate what would be called a "preferential option for the poor." The same expression, echoed by the Second General Conference of Latin American Bishops in Medellín (Colombia) in 1968, was developed in Latin America by theologians Gustavo Gutiérrez and Leonardo Boff, the founders of so-called liberation theology. What does Francis think of liberation theology? Is he also referring to that when he speaks of the "Church of the poor and for the poor"?

Within the Church there have always been great discussions about the poor and so-called liberation, but in the past century, two positions were highlighted that were quite extreme. The first wanted to reduce everything to a Marxist concept and wanted to completely subordinate any reflection on the issue to certain sociological analyses. The other, on the contrary, was suspicious of any social discourse and accused any person who defended the poor of Marxist ideology. The two positions degenerated in Latin America, pushing young people into the arms of the guerrillas or into supporting authoritarian governments and murderers. Cardinal Bergoglio always refused both extremes. Throughout his life, he took the side of the poor and acted strongly against the contempt for the dignity of the outcasts of society. For him, in fact, the poor are the heart of the Church.

As a young man, he had already visited the slums of the city and stopped to talk with ordinary people. He has always done this, and he certainly did not stop when they appointed him cardinal. We all know that he always devoted a lot of time to the priests who worked in the poorest neighborhoods of Buenos Aires and accompanied them during their visits.

At the same time, however, he has always refused to reduce his view of reality to some purely sociological concept. At the General Conference of Latin American Bishops who met together in 2007 at the Shrine of Our Lady of Aparecida in Brazil, from the time they began to prepare the final document, he asked that it would avoid a falsely clinical vision of reality. In fact, a pastor's view is always pastoral. He repeated the same thing in his speech to the bishops of Latin America during his trip to Brazil, and he reaffirmed it in *Evangelii Gaudium*: "Nor would we be well served by a purely sociological analysis which would aim to embrace all of reality by employing an allegedly neutral and clinical method. What I would like to propose is something much more in the line of an evangelical discernment. It is the approach of a missionary disciple" (EG 50).

The most important debate of the last fifty years has focused on what should be the starting point of the Church's consideration. The Church's teachings have always stressed that the faith of the Church, and not the condition of the poor, is the fundamental starting point of the Church's reflections. Francis also says this: "Our faith in Christ, who became poor, and was always close to the poor and the outcast, is the basis of our concern for the integral development of society's most neglected members" (EG 186). Cardinal Bergoglio has never questioned this statement, even though he always thought it seemed insufficient. If Christians are surrounded by the poor, that reality should be foremost in their minds and should be the starting point for their reflection.

So doctrine should not be the sole and exclusive perspective from which we must begin our initial reflection because there are other complementary views that can accompany and enrich the eyes of faith. The situation of the poor is the "immediate inescapable context" of theology in the places where poverty exists. Sitting in comfort while we reflect is not the same thing as constantly being challenged by the suffering of so many poor who are often believing Christians. In this context, we understand the need for a theology that would flow from a condition of strong inequality and marginalization, one that is concerned with the integral liberation of so many sons and daughters of the Church who live lives sunk in misery. So what emerges clearly is the extent to which the Catholic faith can come to promote people's integral development. The document *Libertatis Nuntius*—an instruction that was signed by Cardinal Joseph Ratzinger on August 6, 1984, and focused on some aspects of liberation theology—recalled that "the defenders of orthodoxy are sometimes accused of passivity, indulgence, or culpable complicity regarding the intolerable situations of injustice and the political regimes which prolong them" (XI, 18)—words also quoted by the pope in *Evangelii Gaudium*.

However, one thing is crucial for Francis: in Latin America, the poor are believers, and many of them are Catholics. So, focusing on the poor also means beginning with their faith, their religion, their culture steeped in faith. How we view the poor cannot come merely from a sociopolitical standpoint, and it is not enough just to address their neediness by teaching them to fight, as though we were the bountiful saviors of the ignorant and the simple. If we really have to focus on the poor, we must recognize them as creative, respect where they are coming from, their language, their way of looking at life, their culture, their priorities, and also their religiosity. It makes sense that we have to fight for them, defend their rights, and help them to move forward, but not from outside or from above but from within. Cardinal Bergoglio saw that some liberation theologians did not take these aspects into account, and because of that, he was never very enthusiastic about their proposals. For the same reason, in *Evangelii Gaudium*, he devotes considerable space to the development of a theology and spirituality of the option for the poor, saying that "we need to let ourselves be evangelized by them," embracing "the mysterious wisdom which God wishes to share with us through them" (EG 198). He continues, "This entails appreciating the poor in their goodness, in their experience of life, in their culture, and in their ways of living the faith" (no. 199).

A number of peace movements have emerged that were inspired by the figure of St. Francis of Assisi, some of them formed by nonbelievers. In his pilgrimage to Assisi, the pope claimed not to share the vision of those who believe that peace resides in the search for a certain pantheistic harmony with the energies of the cosmos. He pointed out that there is no true peace without Christ and his cross. And yet St. Francis has something to say even to those who do not believe, so much so that in the past, there were many who, when

asked what name the future pope should take, replied without hesi-
tation: Francis. How can we reconcile these two worlds that refer to
the figure of the saint of Assisi?

The figure of St. Francis of Assisi needs to be completely revised. He is the saint of communion with all creatures in the universe, but he is also the saint of poverty, of brotherhood, of love for the outcasts, of complete union with Jesus Christ, of embracing pain as a form of gift to the Lord. All this is part of the beauty that is the person of Francis. What this pope is doing is restoring all these aspects, without excluding any one of them.

We can see how, in *Evangelii Gaudium*, despite the fact that he refutes pantheism, he does take on some of the tropes of environmental movements and Eastern religions, such as our intimate union with the whole of creation, according to which we cannot understand ourselves fully if we are separate from the rest of creation. He says, "God has joined us so closely to the world around us that we can feel the desertification of the soil almost as a physical ailment, and the extinction of a species as a painful disfigurement" (EG 215).

By expressing it like this, a great ecological vision emerges along with a capacity for dialogue with all those who are passionately committed to these issues. In truth, what worries him most in some of the New Age movements, which have little to do with the Franciscan view, is the development of a lifestyle that is obsessed with health, the search for "energies" to heal ourselves and feel good. This represents an individualistic lifestyle in which one is completely enclosed in one's ego, and that cannot heal the hearts of the people. This is why he devotes so many paragraphs of his document to inviting us to missionary generosity, to service, to the joy of the gift of self. At the same time, Francis highlights the temptation to go no further than shallow, uncommitted religious sentiment. Toward the end of the document, then, he devotes several paragraphs to proposing a spirituality that also gives us a taste for "being a people" (EG 268–74). And so it is much more than simply harmony with nature.

St. Francis left everything to follow Christ. We know that his was a true conversion. It occurred in 1205. While he was praying in the Church of San Damiano, he says that he heard the crucifix speaking to him, and that three times it said, "Francis, go and repair my house which, as you see, is in ruins." Francis took the fabrics from his father's shop and went to Foligno to sell them; he also sold the horse, returned home on foot, and offered the money he had raised to the priest at San Damiano so that he could repair the small church. His father, Peter Bernardone, did not take this well. He felt betrayed by his son. But Francis had already decided. He abandoned everything for Christ: comfort, privileges, wealth.

Fr. Víctor, is it precisely this same dispossession that is asked of every person and of the Church today? This attitude, along with a certain austerity, obviously affects Pope Francis considerably. He goes around in a simple car, dislikes pomp and luxuries, visits refugees, and talks to the poor. In the aforementioned interview with Civiltà Cattolica, he mentioned that he felt close to the mysticism of Louis Lallemant and Jean-Joseph Surin. Both preach the need to "divest ourselves" in order to reach God. Is this the path that Bergoglio will follow?

On this issue, we need to make some subtle distinctions, so that we do not misinterpret the teaching of Pope Francis. He does not love sacrifice for its own sake; nor is he obsessed with austerity. It is more of an inward nakedness, renouncing the habit of focusing too much on oneself, in order to be able to put God and others at the center of one's life. This has a pastoral significance because it implies being more available, closer to the poor, to their limitations, their social status, their humiliations. It is precisely for this reason that Bergoglio does not like flashy priests, or jet-setting bishops, or clerics who wear gold cufflinks, or those who like to be continually visited by powerful people and who are constantly talking about themselves and feel superior to others. All this is nothing but spiritual worldliness, which poisons the Church.

However, I must insist that we not focus solely on the issue of austerity. In the moral and spiritual teaching of the Church, this is part of temperance, which is one of the virtues we do not hear much about. But the most important virtue is love, the gift of love. So, the problem arises especially when the attachment to worldly pleasures closes people within themselves and weakens their generosity and availability. In truth, the pope is not much bothered if priests like to eat well or are distracted with worldly glory, money and other forms of power, because the pope is not annoyed by people wanting to be happy and love life. On the contrary, like any good father, he wants people to suffer as little as possible and enjoy their existence on this earth. In this regard, see what he says in *Evangelii Gaudium*: "We know that God wants his children to be happy in this world too, even though they are called to fulfilment in eternity, for he has created all things 'for our enjoyment' (1 Tim 6:17), the enjoyment of everyone" (EG 182).

A pope who tells us that God wants us to be happy on this earth will never ask us to be obsessed with sacrifice and to seek suffering like masochists, but to share, to serve, to be close to those who are sick, to be available to open the door to others. The problem is the elitist ego. And it is for just that reason, I would maintain, that he completely rejects the privileges of both secular and ecclesiastical authorities. What gives greatest offense is the quest for power, prestige, or luxury in order to feel greater than the others, so that others are in the service of their vanity, while forgetting that the key to power lies in prostrating themselves before others, fighting for the good of others, getting their hands dirty in serving others. He always avoids gossip, but I have heard him sometimes complain about some priests and politicians who are guilty of the sin of self-centeredness, which deforms the mission of service that God has entrusted to them.

Also in Assisi, the pope spoke of spiritual worldliness, a danger that seems primarily to affect the Church. He spoke about it in the Stripping Room in the archbishop's residence, a place that evokes St. Francis's sensational gesture of taking off his rich clothes, a place that no pope had ever entered before. He asked, "What does the Church need to be stripped of?" And he answered, "We must strip ourselves today of a very serious danger that threatens every person in the Church, everyone: the danger of worldliness. The Christian cannot live with the spirit of the world: the worldliness that leads us to vanity, arrogance, and pride. And this is an idol, it is not God. It is an idol! And idolatry is the most serious sin, isn't it?" In what way can the Church free itself of this worldliness?

Pope Francis has explained very well what this terrible form of worldliness is that seizes precisely those who believe they are immune from it. They feel that they are different from and better than others, when in fact they are obsessed with their power and their social status, and this is profoundly worldly. In his magisterial document, he explains this in a way that is raw and direct: "Those who have fallen into this worldliness look on from above and afar, they reject the prophecy of their brothers and sisters, they discredit those who raise questions, they constantly point out the mistakes of others and they are obsessed by appearances. Their hearts are open only to the limited horizon of their own immanence and interests, and as a consequence they neither learn from their sins nor are they genuinely open to forgiveness" (EG 97). It is difficult to read these passages without trembling. The pope is firm, prophetic, and does not show the slightest hesitation when he utters these words. I think anyone who can understand this will also come to discover its positive counterpart: in other words, the way of life that he wants to propose to the faithful, and whose precious symbol is the humble, stripped, free, and generous figure of St. Francis of Assisi.

In Evangelii Gaudium, the pope also speaks of other temptations present in the Church and, in particular, in pastoral workers: an exaggerated concern for their personal areas of autonomy and latitude, egotistical sloth that allows them to carry out all their activities without spirituality, a sterile pessimism as though they feel defeated right from the start when faced with the world, and finally wars of envy and jealousy within the Church itself, among Christians. These seem to be similar temptations to the spiritual worldliness that we just talked about, almost as if it was the source of all these other faults. Is that the case?

Yes, because all the other temptations are only different expressions of this obsession with one's self and with one's false sense of security, one's vanity, one's being closed to anything but one's own interests. Spiritual worldliness is manifested in an excessive confidence in one's abilities, in believing one's own ideas to be absolute, in the habit of judging others, in the permanent war against those who are different, in an individualism of convenience, and in the absence of fervent generosity.

In the Church, spiritual worldliness is aggravated by the fact that it is disguised behind a mask of spirituality, faith, or orthodoxy. As St. Paul says, it is Satan who "masquerades as an angel of light" (2 Cor 11:14). Like the French Jesuit theologian Henri de Lubac, the pope believes that spiritual worldliness is worse than any other sin, precisely because the person is no longer able to recognize his or her weakness and, therefore, is closed to conversion. Behind the appearance of good, the heart remains closed to the saving action of God.

Let's stay on the subject of Bergoglio's choice of Francis as his name. A retrospective recently came out that claimed that if he had been elected pope in 2005, he would have called himself John XXIV. This, in fact, is what Bergoglio as the future Francis explained to Cardinal Francis Marchisano, from Piedmont, on the occasion of the election of Ratzinger. At that time, Marchisano was archpriest of St. Peter's Basilica. Beyond the veracity or otherwise of this backstory, is Angelo Roncalli the pope who inspires Bergoglio's pontificate? And, in particular, in your opinion, what does Francis think of Vatican II? It is said that after years of trying to give a conservative or liberal slant to the Council (the great "battles" over hermeneutics), he believes that the time has come to "implement" the Council. Is that so?

Francis is very different from the popes who preceded him, although it is true that he may have characteristics of one or the other. The most important thing is that he always follows the way that the Council has opened up. Undoubtedly, he prefers to stay out of theoretical discussions about the Council, because what interests him is continuing in the same spirit of renewal and reform. In this respect, he remains on the margins of the obsession with ideology. Rather, he applies the Council in its entirety, with no gaps or backtracking, with the intention of leading the Church out of itself, until it is completely implemented. This also applies to many paths of reform that were opened by the Council but were interrupted midway. For example, there has never been a concrete development of the importance that the Council gave to collegiality and episcopal conferences. Indeed, the trend was increasingly to remove power from local bodies.

2

Innovations Emerging from *Evangelii Gaudium*

On March 4, 1979, John Paul II published his first encyclical, *Redemptor Hominis*. It was, in effect, his pontifical program and can be summed up using just one word: *Christ*. Christ, the Word of God made man; Christ, the only model of behavior; Christ, the object and foundation of faith. Christ, therefore, is the key to understanding Karol Wojtyla, but not just that. Christ is the foundation of the entire life of John Paul II. He himself wrote in the same encyclical, "The only guidance of the Spirit, the only direction for our intellect, will and heart for us is this: toward Christ, the Redeemer of humanity; toward Christ, the Redeemer of the world. We want to look to Him, because only in Him, the Son of God, is salvation" (no. 7). It was on April 20, 2005, when, in his first message at the end of the Eucharistic concelebration with the cardinals who had elected him in the Sistine Chapel, Pope Benedict XVI spoke of the plan for his own pontificate: to implement the Second Vatican Council, "following in the footsteps of my predecessors and in faithful continuity with the 2,000-year tradition of the Church," he said, and "to work tirelessly to rebuild the full and visible unity of all Christ's followers." These were two major fundamental commitments that did not, however, prevent him from saying a few days later that, in addition to them, his "real program of governance is not to do my own will, not to pursue my own ideas, but to listen, together with the whole Church, to the word and will of the Lord, to be guided by Him, so that He himself will lead the Church at this hour of our history." In short, just as it was for Wojtyla, so it was for Joseph Ratzinger: above everything, he was anchored to Christ, to his person and to his will.

And what about Francis? He himself said that the whole of *Evangelii Gaudium* "has a programmatic meaning" (EG 25). His is a call to a profound renewal. In the wake of Paul VI's encyclical *Ecclesiam Suam*, which explained how "the Church must look with penetrating eyes within itself, ponder the mystery of its own being....A vivid and lively self-awareness on the part of the Church inevitably leads to a comparison between the ideal image of the Church as Christ envisaged it, His holy and spotless bride, and the actual image which the Church presents to the world today.... Hence the Church's heroic and impatient struggle for renewal: the struggle to correct those flaws introduced by its members which its own self-examination, mirroring its exemplar, Christ, points out to it and condemns" (*Ecclesiam Suam* 9–11). This is, therefore, the Church reforming itself through faithfulness to Christ. And for Francis too, the rock to lean on is Christ, his person. It is only in Christ, Francis seems to say, that the Church can renew itself and that his pontificate can have a purpose.

Fr. Víctor, let's start with the title. What does it mean? Why was the exhortation called Evangelii Gaudium?

Regarding the title, we have to distinguish two things that can be helpful to us in the interpretation of the whole document. In the main title, what stands out is the word *gaudium*, because it has the word *evangelii* in common with another document that the pope has very much at heart: Pope Paul VI's *Evangelii*

Nuntiandi. By naming it in this way, Francis wanted to show us his intention to take up the challenges of Giovanni Battista Montini's document, but to present those challenges in a new light, however, and updated for the world of today. The emphasis on *gaudium*, "joy," is an antidote to the disenchantment and melancholy of the world today. Pope Francis wants to instill in the Church a wave of joy and enthusiasm. However, the subtitle contains a clarification: the issue is not evangelization in general, but the "announcement" of the Gospel. Evangelization is something broader and would require other more specific issues relating to the activities of the Church to be addressed. Nor is it the Church's teaching. For the Church to conform itself more and more to the image of joyful and fervent announcer of this message of life and joy, it must be transformed, renewed, and reformed.

It is no secret to anyone that Lumen Fidei, *Pope Francis's first encyclical, draws in part from a contribution that had already been written by Benedict XVI, just as it is no mystery that sometimes even popes ask for help from others in preparing their documents. Thus, for example, we know that many of the texts written by John Paul II were drafted with the wise advice of the then prefect of the Congregation for the Doctrine of the Faith, Cardinal Ratzinger himself. Are you aware of who participated in, or even contributed to, the drafting of* Evangelii Gaudium?

I believe that, as often happens, the Holy Father may have asked for help in developing some points. But in *Evangelii Gaudium*, any help he received from the outside seems to have had little relevance because on every page of the document, it is his style that emerges, his language, his concerns, and his major themes. The topics and the way they are treated are undoubtedly his. What we can say is that the contributions received from other people were only subsidiary because the voice that comes across is undoubtedly from him alone. In the encyclical *Lumen Fidei*, we can clearly see the hand of Benedict XVI. Here, instead, it is Francis who shines through the text.

It is easy to see that most of the document consists of previous texts by the same pope, texts from before he became pope. However, the issues are extensively reworked in the document and placed inside a homogeneous structure. For example, the famous "four principles" that can also be found in many of his previous writings ("time is greater than space," "unity prevails over conflict," "realities are more important than ideas," and "the whole is greater than the part") are also present in *Evangelii Gaudium*. However, in this document, they are placed in the context of building peace in society with a very precise objective and are explained more clearly (see EG 221). On the other hand, other topics are raised that are drawn from his experience as a pope who now has before him the horizon of the whole world. In this sense, there are themes that cover a new and universal dimension, especially the concern for world peace, dialogue with the other great religions, world economy, and the reform of the Church. All this flows from his heart as the universal pastor guided by the Spirit and cannot have been simply a contribution from an adviser.

In the last chapter of the document, the pope quotes some paragraphs from your writings, Fr. Víctor. Had he spoken to you about this?

He simply informed me that he would quote a few paragraphs from my writings. How did he know about them? It stands to reason that, prior to appointing me rector of his university, he would have read some of the things I had written, in order to avoid surprises! He always devotes a considerable amount of time to reading, especially in the early morning and after sunset. I imagine that, in one of those moments, he took note of those paragraphs and then decided to include them in the document.

Why? Because they are not just an expression of my thoughts so much as an expression of ideas that are very common in Argentina and South America.

How important is it to you that the pope decided to include those quotes?

With all due respect, I think that he would have expressed the same things a lot better if he had used his own language, which is so creative and evocative. He had no need to quote me. However, I think it is a gesture that indicates that Francis welcomes theological and spiritual reflections that come from the ends of the earth and not just from countries that are considered the center of the world. In this sense, there is something of immense value that should not go unnoticed: one of the great innovations of this document is that it welcomes the contributions of local bishops. He quotes documents from the Bishops Conferences in Congo, the Philippines, India, the United States, Oceania, and so on. And that's not all; he also quotes the laity from Catholic Action in Italy. I do not remember a papal document that has ever been so inclusive. This is in fact a great innovation! It shows that the pope thinks about the whole of the universal Church, listening to everyone, trying to express the anguish, the hopes, and the riches of all.

A document like Evangelii Gaudium, *consisting of over 200 pages in 288 paragraphs, cannot be summarized in a few words. It is a huge document, one that opens up horizons instead of closing them, and that answers many questions while also asking new ones. Nevertheless, how would you summarize its contents? What is at the heart of the document, its central idea?*

Right from the beginning, *Evangelii Gaudium* proposes a path of joy, the enjoyment of opening oneself to the Lord and doing good, with the aim of reviving the spirit of the Church and of the people who work and struggle for noble purposes. He reminds Christians that "Jesus can also break through the dull categories with which we would enclose him and he constantly amazes us by his divine creativity. Whenever we make the effort to return to the source and to recover the original freshness of the Gospel, new avenues arise, new paths of creativity open up" (EG 11).

The first chapter is a proposal to reform the missionary character of the whole Church, where he reminds us that "the papacy and the central structures of the universal Church also need to hear the call to pastoral conversion" (EG 32). However, he adds that the way in which the message is presented must be thoroughly revised, so that it reaches "everyone without exception or exclusion" (no. 35). And he asks us not to place so much emphasis on secondary issues, but that the gospel proclamation be focused on the essentials, that there be a "sense of proportion" and of placing things in their proper context (no. 38). In addition, he mentions some customs within the Church that no longer provide the same service as before in terms of the transmission of the gospel message, and he asks that we be not "afraid to re-examine them" (no. 43). He proposes a Church that has open doors, and he is not only talking about churches, but also referring to the sacraments.

The second chapter provides a survey of the reality of today. And it is there that he expresses himself in prophetic language. He harshly criticizes the trickle-down effect that does not take responsibility for those who are excluded from society, and he rails against having a "crude and naïve trust in the goodness of those wielding economic power and in the sacralized workings of the prevailing economic system" (EG 54). He also points the finger at the obsession with security that is demanded without worrying about the causes of failure: "When a society—whether local, national or global—is willing to leave a part of itself on the fringes, no political programs or resources spent on law enforcement or surveillance systems can indefinitely guarantee tranquility" (no. 59). Another novelty of his analysis of reality is the amount of space he devotes to the defects and the temptations of those who hold office within the Church. He is very incisive in emphasizing such temptations, especially spiritual worldliness, the attachment to ways of doing things in the past or the rigidity of certain doctrines, and the quest for power, glory, or money within the Church itself.

The third chapter focuses on the proclamation of the Gospel. He rejects elitist Christianity and calls for the participation of everyone, recognizing the role of the poor and the simple as active members and not merely objects of the Church's action. He also focuses largely on proposing that priests prepare their homilies more attentively, because "there are many complaints leveled against this important ministry" and he recognizes that the faithful suffer greatly when they hear the sermons of some priests (EG 35).

The fourth chapter develops the social dimension of evangelization and the social consequences of faith. In a deep and thoughtful way, he reopens the issue of the option for the poor and insists again on the need for a different economy, one that resolves the structural causes of poverty. However, together with the issue of the poor, his concern for social peace also emerges, both in the world at large and in each individual country. He proposes an interesting and elaborate way of building peace in society, based on his original four principles. In the end, with considerable respect and openness, he launches several new proposals aimed at dialogue between the Church and non-Catholics.

In the last chapter, he explains how major changes are not possible when a spirit and attitude that mobilize people are absent. So, he pauses to explain the motivations that could lead to a new commitment that is full of strength and enthusiasm. These are issues that I hope to cover in more depth in the course of this conversation.

From the beginning of his pontificate, Pope Francis has amazed everyone with his ability to synthesize—and not only that, but also with the brevity of his speeches and the concepts he expresses in them. The morning homilies in St. Martha's House, for example, are as effective as they are brief. By using a few concrete examples, he manages to get his point across to his audience, even though these same sermons almost never last more than five minutes. The pope, in short, has very quickly made us become accustomed to short and incisive sentences. In Evangelii Gaudium, *on the other hand, he presents us with a long document in which the issues are developed extensively. So which is Bergoglio's true style?*

Besides being full of incisive and stimulating phrases, *Evangelii Gaudium* develops thoughtfully and argumentatively, and this shows how "our" Francis, whom we think of as simple and close to us, is also a great thinker who is able to communicate what we most need to hear at this moment in history. By doing so, he refutes the criticisms from certain persons, some of whom are high up in the Church, who have said that he is a person of little depth, who lacks the ability to reflect on issues. However, true to his own style, in this document, Pope Francis gets his point across with sentences or short sections that will go down in history as examples of text in which he shows his capacity for using only a few words to say things that are very complex and that challenge us deeply.

What are the most significant paragraphs, in your opinion?

For the time being, I will mention a few that impressed me because of their passionate sincerity, only because, in my opinion, they lay bare the heart of the pope:

No one can strip us of the dignity bestowed upon us by this boundless and unfailing love....Let us not flee from the resurrection of Jesus, let us never give up, come what will. (EG 3)

I prefer a Church which is bruised, hurting and dirty because it has been out on the streets, rather than a Church which is unhealthy from being confined and from clinging to its own security. I do not want a Church concerned with being at the center and which then ends by being caught up in a web of obsessions and procedures. (EG 49)

It always pains me greatly to discover how some Christian communities, and even consecrated persons, can tolerate different forms of enmity, division, calumny, defamation, vendetta, jealousy and the desire to impose certain ideas at all costs, even to persecutions which appear as veritable witch hunts. Whom are we going to evangelize if this is the way we act? (EG 100)

This infamous network of crime is now well established in our cities, and many people have blood on their hands as a result of their comfortable and silent complicity. (EG 211)

One of the more serious temptations which stifles boldness and zeal is a defeatism which turns us into querulous and disillusioned pessimists, "sourpusses." (EG 85)

Frequently, we act as arbiters of grace rather than its facilitators. But the Church is not a tollhouse; it is the house of the Father, where there is a place for everyone, with all their problems. (EG 47)

We have already mentioned this above, but it's worth coming back to. A key document for the life of the Church in Latin America is the final text of the Fifth Conference of the Latin American Bishops at Aparecida (São Paulo) held in 2007. That document was prepared, for the first time, from the ground up. The General Conference, in short, did not start from a prepackaged base text but from open dialogue that had already begun beforehand among the bishops of Latin America and that then continued. Also, this was the first time a Latin American Bishops' Conference had met at a Marian shrine. This emphasized the sense of belonging to the faithful, the Church going forward as the people of God, and the bishops as his servants. The document, then, was not an end in itself, it was not the last step, because in the end, it opened onto the mission of the Church: the proclamation and the witness of the disciples. Cardinal Bergoglio said the following during an interview with the magazine 30Days: *"To remain faithful we must come out of ourselves. It is through remaining faithful that we can come out. This is basically what* Aparecida *says. It is the heart of our mission." Fr. Víctor, what is the relationship between* Evangelii Gaudium *and the* Aparecida Document *that is so dear to Pope Francis?*

There are two important subjects in *Evangelii Gaudium* that also received a lot of space in *Aparecida*. One is the need to dedicate oneself to pastoral workers in order to give them strength amid the temptations of the world today. The other is the commitment to lead the Church toward a missionary "openness." *Aparecida* recognized the problem of the loss of fervor on the part of pastoral workers. Today we live with a constant and suffocating supply of consumerism that offers us new cellphones, laptops, PDAs, accessories of all kinds, a wide variety of food and places to eat, an infinite number of television series, travel, beaches, and so forth. At the same time, in order to take advantage of all these things, people want more free time. It follows that life tends to make us more and more private and that people begin to make choices that allow them to take more advantage of their time, and therefore they opt for anything that provides gratification for their senses or their ego. The result is the sadness of self-centeredness, which flows from a heart that becomes more comfortable and avaricious day by day. To remind us that by following this path, there will be less life instead of more life, we read in *Aparecida*, "Life grows by being given away, and it weakens in isolation and comfort. Indeed, those who enjoy life most are those who leave security on the shore and become excited by in [*sic*] the mission of communicating life to others" (AD 360).

When you ask the pope how he can have increased energy, physical strength, initiative, and enthusiasm, he replies, "Here I have things to entertain me." But we must not understand this sentence in a superficial way; it means "I have a lot to do. And I have both the responsibility and the freedom to do it." In truth, each of us could say the same thing. This confirms that we don't need to cut down on our activities or live on the defensive in order to be strong and healthy. On the contrary, if our gift of self is sincere, generous, and joyful, Christ will always continue to renew us, even if we are elderly. As we find written in the Bible, "But those who wait for the LORD shall renew their strength, they shall mount up with wings like eagles, they shall run and not be weary, they shall walk and not faint" (Isa 40:31). The pope teaches us that every time we try to go back to the source and regain our original freshness, new paths spring up.

For Bergoglio, *Aparecida* has also meant a powerful rediscovery of the missionary vocation of the Church, of the need to return to the idea of the Church being on the move. This is what John Paul II wrote in *Redemptoris Missio*, in which he reminds us that the proclamation of the Gospel to those who are far away "is the first task of the Church" (RM 34), that missionary activity is "the greatest challenge for the Church" (no. 40), and that "the missionary task must remain foremost" (no. 86). When John Paul II spoke these words, we did not listen to him as we should have. Instead, *Aparecida* took seriously the fact that going out to look for those who are far away is the model for the whole work of the Church. It is what in Latin America is called the "missionary paradigm." It means that the whole task of the Church, although not always addressed to those who are distant geographically, must have an attitude of "going out."

This is what Pope Francis repeats on every occasion. Similarly, *Aparecida* emphasized that "we cannot passively and calmly wait in our church buildings" (AD 548) and that we have to move "from a pastoral ministry of mere conservation to a decidedly missionary pastoral ministry" (no. 370). This task continues to be one of the greatest sources of joy for the Church: "There will be more joy in heaven over one sinner who repents than over ninety-nine righteous persons who need no repentance" (Luke 15:7). For Bergoglio, *Aparecida* was a rediscovery of the Church that not only evangelizes but is essentially missionary, that is, necessarily "outside," geared toward all those on the periphery who need the light of the Gospel. Some Brazilian bishops were affected by this concern for a new strongly missionary phase and were concerned about the decline of the faithful in their country. Among them, Cardinal Cláudio Hummes (then prefect of the Congregation for the Clergy) was very insistent on this issue.

The *Aparecida Document* is not a great work of literature. There was, in fact, little time to review it, and therefore, it is full of repetitions and is partly disordered and heterogeneous. However, it expresses the results of a great debate and today plays an important strategic role. When Cardinal Bergoglio returned to Buenos Aires from Aparecida, he began to stress these issues more than ever. He addressed himself to priests, catechists, and all Christians, talking constantly of the need for permanent mission. He invited his auxiliary bishops to be creative in finding new ways to convey the love of Christ to all the faithful of the diocese, and he himself began to "go out" much more than before. Today, these issues contained in *Aparecida* have become an integral part of his papal plan.

3

First the Gospel, Then the Principles

For many observers, Francis is the pope of mercy. He does not deny any of the Church's doctrine—he will not change that—but his approach on such ethically sensitive subjects as the most controversial issues in the relationship between the Church and the world is never one of condemnation but always of openness, of acceptance—so much so that, from the first months of his pontificate, the words that come to mind are those written by another Jesuit, Marko Rupnik, director of the Ezio Aletti Research Center, in his book *Il Rosso della Piazza d'Oro*: "People change when they feel loved, not when they see themselves humiliated or constrained. God expects our sacrifice to be free, made with love and for love, and not because we are obligated. The angry reaction of rejection facing Christianity in many parts of Europe expresses the need not for permissiveness or indifference or a retreat through fear, but an offering of love and fellowship that awakens desire and leaves space for free membership."

In essence, it is a bit like what Francis himself said in an interview with *La Civiltà Cattolica*: "We cannot focus only on issues related to abortion, gay marriage and the use of contraceptive methods. This is not possible. I have not spoken much about these things, and I was reprimanded for it. But when we speak about these things, we have to speak about them in a context. We know what the Church's opinion on these things is and I am a son of the Church, but it is not necessary to talk about them all the time."

The teaching that the pope wants to give seems, after all, simple and altogether new. The missionary ministry, the Church's approach to the world, to nonbelievers, in the first place, cannot focus on a set of doctrines to be imposed as a matter of urgency because, all things being equal, what attracts are love and mercy, which is then the heart of the good news brought into the world by Jesus Christ. In summary, one could say that Francis is the pope who puts the announcement of the gospel message before the principles, an embrace before a condemnation. Or, to use the words of an editorial that *La Civiltà Cattolica* dedicated to Francis in the edition that came out shortly before Christmas 2013, "Pope Francis loves faces more than ideas." That is, above all, he loves people, their stories, their lives. And he places nothing in the way of that love—neither prejudice nor ideology.

Fr. Víctor, the media around the world praise the "openness" of Francis and are amazed more than anything that he does not insist primarily on principles but, as he himself said in the interview granted to La Civiltà Cattolica *on September 19, 2013, on "what makes the heart burn, as it did for the disciples at Emmaus"; in short, on the essentials, on the Gospel. Is this the fundamental characteristic, the heart of the new pontificate?*

The announcement of the heart of the Gospel before anything else is an important feature of Francis. However, this must be understood in the context of a renewal of the Church's mission. The pope believes that a Church that wants to come out of itself and reach everyone must necessarily change its way of preaching. He invites us to recognize that, many times, the precepts of the moral teaching of the Church are presented outside of the context that gives them meaning. The biggest problem occurs when the message that the Church proclaims is identified only with those aspects that do not fully represent the heart of the message of Jesus Christ. A missionary ministry cannot be obsessed with the transmission of a disjointed set of doctrines that purports to impose them by forcefully insisting on them. When the Church adopts a missionary style through which it wants to reach everyone, without exceptions or exclusions, the proclamation focuses on what is most beautiful, great, and attractive and, at the same time, most necessary.

Certainly, all the truths of Christianity affirm the same faith, but some of them are more important because they express in a more direct way the fundamental core that is "the beauty of the saving love of God manifested in Jesus Christ" (EG 36). The Gospel, in particular, invites us to respond to the redeeming love of God by recognizing it in others, seeking the good of all. This invitation should not be overshadowed by anything! The pope said that if this invitation does not shine strongly and attractively, the morality of the Church runs the risk of becoming a house of cards, and this is our greatest danger. The message loses its freshness and stops having "the fragrance of the Gospel" (no. 39).

The other side of the pope's own style emerges, which not only focuses on what is essential but also expresses it clearly and with powerful gestures. Judging by the effect it is having, we can only look positively on this style, although it can be annoying to some who are in the minority and are not representative of the Church at large.

When the pope comes across like that, it becomes clear to us that he is not naïve. He invites us to immerse ourselves in the context of today's culture in a very realistic way. He invites us to recognize that the speed of communication and the selection of the content offered by the media confront us with a new challenge. Often the gospel message can appear mutilated, and the message that we proclaim ends up identifying with only these minor points. When that happens, we only reach a few people who identify with certain specific issues. Instead, if we adopted a missionary style that can really reach everyone, the proclamation would focus on the essentials which, at the same time, is what is most attractive because it responds to the deepest needs of the human heart. In doing so, the pope has taken to heart the teaching of the Second Vatican Council: the "hierarchy of truths" (UR 11).

The "hierarchy of truths" of the faith is a theme that is very dear to Francis. Following the teaching of the Church, he believes that catechesis must take this hierarchy into account at all levels. He believes that with catechesis, we can highlight the essential contents of the Christian message, not only so that we can surround them with all the truths of the faith, but also so that we can make the various life situations of believers shine with their light: the core (kerygma) of the Christian message inspires and nourishes the faith of the baptized and makes it able to be embodied in different cultures and human situations. But can we better explain what this hierarchy of the truths of the faith means for the theology of the Church, and what it means in a particular way for Pope Francis?

It is a central theme, and I would say it is the key to understand the teaching and the choices of this pope. So thank you for that question because it allows me to focus on this subject and to explain it in detail. I think we need to point out different aspects that help us to understand the richness and challenges inherent in the concept of the hierarchy of truths.

First, one must focus on the "heart" of the Gospel: "In this basic core, what shines forth is the beauty of the saving love of God made manifest in Jesus Christ who died and rose from the dead" (EG 36). Second, it should be recognized that other truths are connected to this heart in different ways, some more directly than others. It follows that the truths are not all equally important, precisely "since they vary in their relation to the fundamental Christian faith" (UR 11). This applies as much to the dogmas of the faith as to all the teachings of the Church, including the moral teaching. The pope reminds us that "Saint Thomas Aquinas taught that the Church's moral teaching has its own 'hierarchy,' in the virtues and in the acts which proceed from them" and that "works of love directed to one's neighbor are the most perfect external manifestation of the interior grace of the Spirit" (EG 37). Consequently, some truths express the core of the Gospel in a more direct way, others indirectly. All revealed truths proceed from the same divine source and are believed with the same faith, but some are more important because they express more directly the heart of the Gospel. All this has pastoral consequences.

First, we need to stress that in proclaiming the Gospel, it is essential that there be proper proportion, a "new balance," as pointed out by the pope during his interview with *La Civiltà Cattolica*. This proportion is related to the emphases that arise in preaching, which must lean more on the side of the central truths than on secondary ones, more on those that express the heart of the Gospel directly than on those that are connected in a more indirect way. This proportion is also related to the frequency with which we reference and develop these themes. The pope explains it clearly: "If in the course of the liturgical year a parish priest speaks about temperance ten times but only mentions charity or justice two or three times, an imbalance results, and precisely those virtues which ought to be most present in preaching and catechesis are overlooked. The same thing happens when we speak more about law than about grace, more about the Church than about Christ, more about the pope than about God's word" (EG 38).

However, the pope also reminds us that all this presupposes that "just as the organic unity existing among the virtues means that no one of them can be excluded from the Christian ideal, so no truth may be denied. The integrity of the gospel message must not be deformed" (EG 39). Proportion is not mutilation and does not mean completely silencing some truths. In that sense, I have read some unfair criticism of the pope. For example, he never said that we should not speak of true marriage. He has firmly stated that the union between two people of the same sex does not correspond to the ideal of marriage inherent in God's plan. He has been very categorical, especially regarding the defense of life from conception to its natural end. But he has asked us not to mention these issues "exclusively" and "every time," precisely so as not to wear people out and thus produce a negative effect, because these issues are not the heart of the Gospel, which, on the other hand, should be announced constantly and in different ways.

The hierarchy of virtues also implies that all truth is better understood "when related to the harmonious totality of the Christian message; in this context all of the truths are important and illumine one another" (EG 39). This assumes that no truth is denied or hidden, but especially that we never isolate one truth from others that can help us understand it better. This is especially the case when it comes to a truth that is secondary or peripheral, where isolating it from the rest would mean taking away its attractiveness and, above all, taking away its Christian meaning. Isolated secondary truths do not exist in the Gospel. When they are isolated, they become "doctrinal or moral points based on specific ideological options" (EG 39). The pope has told us that we should not be obsessed with the "disjointed transmission of a multitude of doctrines" (EG 35). This implies that there must be a certain structure, or an "order" that is necessary for us to be able to listen and admire. We must be able to recognize and to transmit this network of relationships between the truths, so that it shows more and more the harmony of the whole.

Christian truths should be understood in their relation to each other and even more in relation to the central truth: the infinite love of God who calls us into friendship with him, who offers salvation and life. At the same time, as a moral message, "the Gospel invites us to respond to the God of love who saves us, to see God in others and to go forth from ourselves to seek the good of others. Under no circumstance can this invitation be obscured! All of the virtues are at the service of this response of love" (EG 39).

Finally, the hierarchy of truths invites us to distinguish between the non-negotiable content and the form of expression we use to describe it, because it is precisely the form of expression that can make a secondary subject appear central. Of course, if one wants to feel secure about the doctrine itself, then one can repeat phrases that no one can understand. We must never forget that "the substance is one thing…and the form of expression we use to describe it is another" (John XXIII). The pope has written that "there are times when the faithful, in listening to completely orthodox language, take away something alien to the authentic gospel of Jesus Christ, because that language is alien to their own way of speaking to and understanding one another. With the holy intent of communicating the truth about God and humanity, we sometimes give them a false god or a human ideal which is not really Christian. In this way, we hold fast to a formulation while failing to convey its substance. This is the greatest danger" (EG 41). The pope then repeats the teaching of John Paul II: "The expression of truth can take different forms. The renewal of these forms of expression becomes necessary for the sake of transmitting to the people of today the Gospel message in its unchanging meaning" (UUS 19).

What does it mean to put things in context when it comes to moral issues?

As the pope has said, the moral issues we are talking about must be contextualized so that they can be fully understood. This presupposes that we have a more relevant and wider context, as we shall see.

The broadest context is the kerygma; it is the invitation to an encounter with a God who loves and saves and, because of this, can offer us a better life. This, says the pope, is the meaning of "making the heart burn within us," and it is the most important thing. When the Church talks excessively about philosophical issues or natural law, it does so presumably in order to talk about moral issues with the unbelieving world. However, in doing so, on the one hand, we will never convince anyone using philosophical arguments from the past, and on the other, we miss out on an opportunity to proclaim the beauty of Jesus Christ, to make hearts burn. So, philosophical arguments do not change anyone's life. Instead, if we manage to make their hearts burn, or at least show what is attractive in the Gospel, then people will be more likely to talk and think also about a response that is inherently moral.

However, there should also be a relevant context that should always be something positive about what you are proposing or theorizing. For example, it is no good speaking against homosexual marriage, because people tend to view us as resentful, cruel, exclusive, or even exaggerating the issue. Another aspect is that when we talk about the beauty of marriage and the harmony that is created by the difference resulting from the covenant between a man and a woman, in this context, the positive emerges, almost without having to point it out, whereas it is inappropriate to use the same term and call the union of two homosexuals "marriage."

The Church in Italy, as well as several bishops' conferences in Europe and especially on the North American continent, has had years of conflict in defense of the principles that, in 2006, Benedict XVI called "non-negotiable." Specifically, it was when he had an audience with the participants at the Conference organized by the European People's Party in the Vatican that Benedict XVI summed these principles: protection of life in all its stages, from the first moment of conception until natural death; the recognition and promotion of the natural structure of the family as a union between a man and a woman founded on marriage and its defense in the face of attempts to make it juridically equivalent to radically different forms of union that, in reality, harm it and contribute to its destabilization, obscuring its particular character and its irreplaceable social role; and the protection of the right of parents to educate their children.

These conflicts become so central to the relationship between Catholicism and the opinions that are dominant because the beliefs of the Church come into conflict with many of the beliefs that are to be found in today's society—for example, abortion, euthanasia, and bioethical research. What does Francis think of this?

By misrepresenting the teaching of Benedict XVI, some have gone so far as to say that those non-negotiable principles form the basis and the source of all the teaching of the Church. Now that's a heresy! To maintain that Jesus Christ, his resurrection, brotherly love, and all the Gospel teaches us depend on certain ethical principles is a distortion that deforms the face of Christianity.

For example, the pope is firm in his opposition to abortion, because if you do not defend the innocence of human life, there are not many other arguments that you can use in defense of human rights. It is clear that this is non-negotiable, but it cannot be said that a few moral principles are the light from which flow all the other truths of the faith and of Christianity. The heart of our faith, which illuminates everything, is not this, but the kerygma. This is the only way in which we can understand the powerful role played by the hierarchy of truths that this pope has wanted to reinstate. The problem is that the fanatics end up converting some principles into a lifelong battle and deliberately discuss only those issues.

In addition, some want us to believe that what the pope says is what we have been saying all along, that in fact nothing has changed and that, therefore, we should not feel challenged. This is not so, because he is asking us to adopt a particular style, a sense of proportion, and special emphases. There are two reasons why the pope asks us not to talk about certain moral principles "all the time" and "exclusively": so that we do not wear out our listeners by reaching saturation point and thus suffering rejection, and above all, so that we do not destroy the harmony of our message. Some of the most extremist elements in the Church ridicule the pope, saying, "Now the pope forbids us to talk about these issues." This is a lie, and also slandering the pope is immoral. They are moral when they talk about issues that affect them, but not about other subjects. Some people go so far as to fabricate false accusations in order to ruin the reputation of other people in order to silence those who do not think like them. That too is immoral. It seems that all of a sudden these people have lost all their moral conscience. I believe that some sectors of the Catholic world, which are full of hatred, are unprincipled, and I say this with sadness in my heart because I always value and defend these same principles.

We need only look at how, until two years ago, some people would not have accepted any kind of discussion about the pope's remarks, but now they are engaged in writing and spreading all kinds of criticism of Pope Francis. This is not an outlook of faith, but an ideological battle: I will only defend the pope if he supports what I think. It is true that they can take advantage of the freedom that this pope gives everyone. He does not expect us to repeat uncritically everything he says, but for that same reason, we cannot impose complete uniformity of thought: "For those who long for a monolithic body of doctrine guarded by all and leaving no room for nuance, this might appear as undesirable and leading to confusion. But in fact such variety serves to bring out and develop different facets of the inexhaustible riches of the Gospel" (EG 40).

One last point I should mention is that, although we have to consider each issue case by case, there are other issues that are non-negotiable: love your neighbor, do justice to the oppressed, be honest in our dealing with others, and so forth.

Some opposition to the pope is internal to Catholicism and comes from sources that do not compromise on principles. In this sense, these people seem to go far beyond Benedict XVI, who, while speaking often about them, did not use those principles as a club to beat those who do not adhere to them. On this subject, Francis has reminded us about the risk to the faith when it becomes entrenched in principles and turns into an ideology. Is this opposition a problem for Francis or not? How does he experience criticism from within? How does he view it? And how does he react to it?

He once told me that he was a sinner, that he had many defects and had made many mistakes, and yet he thanked God for having been given a great capacity for suffering and for resilience: a very high pain threshold. Nothing knocks him down. You could also apply his famous second principle in this case, according to which "time is greater than space." He waits, endures, bears the burden because he knows that in time good and truth will triumph.

On the other hand, when he understands clearly that God is calling, this belief overcomes any fatigue, difficulty, and distress he is asked to bear. I heard him say that you should never be naïve, but you should always know how to forgive. He works like this, holding out his hand. He never lets himself be deceived or used, but he is able to embrace and give space to those who have injured him. To me this has great worth because it shows his great consistency with the "culture of encounter" that he invites us to engage in. He invites us always to sacrifice ourselves, to renounce, to overcome our passions, to go beyond ourselves. For the same reason, he is in no hurry to start a reform of the Roman Curia, and he wants this reform to be smooth. He knows that to impose reform from above could mean that the next pope could cancel it out, and he prefers to start from consensus and agreement, so that the reform may last. He also wants certain subjects to be discussed in depth in the synods, so that key issues will gradually emerge that can then be transformed into effective change.

Most conservatives within the Church often criticize him and ridicule him and, by doing so, do not act with the same spirit of faith and love that he teaches us. They find it hard to accept the idea that the Holy Spirit is leading the Church toward a different phase. However, viewing things with the eyes of faith does not mean just tolerating this pope until he passes away, like those who hope that a nasty spell of bad weather will soon pass. Instead, what we have to do is understand what God wants to teach us now through him, even though sometimes it does not look very attractive to us.

In recent years, there have been some who have placed a strong emphasis on doctrinal security, on the honor of the Church and its self-preservation, and who felt they were represented by some Church authorities. To be honest, those who had a plan that was even slightly different from what happened in the past, like Cardinal Bergoglio and many others, were very respectful of these choices, or at least they bore with them in silence. But now I feel that there are some sectors within the Church who feel threatened by the speeches and the style of Francis, and it seems that suddenly they have lost all the affection they felt toward the figure of the pope. I have much respect for those other "conservatives" who instead show more consistency and, even if they feel forced to contradict their own inclinations, maintain a spiritual vision and welcome Pope Francis's proposals.

First the Gospel: that is, the encounter with Christ and his message. Jesus Christ is obviously the center of Francis's life, as well as his being a priest, a pastor, and a pope. According to Pope Francis, what is the characteristic of the person of Christ that the Church should follow the most?

In his document, the pope gives a description of Jesus Christ that is taken directly from the Gospel and says that "Jesus' whole life, his way of dealing with the poor, his actions, his integrity, his simple daily acts of generosity, and finally his complete self-giving, is precious and reveals the mystery of his divine life. Whenever we encounter this anew, we become convinced that it is exactly what others need" (EG 265). This is nothing more than the Jesus of the Gospel, the transparent Gospel, which does not need to be further embellished. Jesus ate and drank with sinners (Matt 11:19), played with the children of his village (Mark 10:13–16).

He could stop to have a conversation with the Samaritan woman (John 4) or with Nicodemus (John 3). He allowed prostitutes to wash his feet (Luke 7:36–50) and stopped to touch the sick with his own saliva (Mark 7:33). When he spoke to someone, he did not listen half-heartedly but gazed at them with a look of attention and love (Mark 10:21). This is the Christ that the pope likes, and he is the one that the pope holds up to us as an example to be followed by the whole Church.

However, he never hesitates to go all the way and say that in Christ, everything is aimed at the "the glory of the Father which Jesus sought at every moment of his life. As the Son, he rejoices eternally to be 'close to the Father's heart' (Jn 1:18)" (LEG 267). The pope does not want to disfigure the image of Jesus because he knows that in his human embrace, we also need to find his divine power that can sustain our lives. Jesus is the model of a human being, but he is also the Savior. He is the poor child of Bethlehem, but he is also the Christ of Easter who redeems us with his blood and fills us with life in his resurrection. He is a close friend and neighbor, yet he is also the glorious Lord who is clothed in infinite light that can strengthen us in all our weakness.

_____

Some believe that in relegating principles to the background, we run the risk of providing excuses for those who believe that the principles are optional and that one may very well ignore them in the name of an existence marked by what Benedict XVI called the "dictatorship of relativism." In other words, doesn't the Church run the risk of embracing the so-called weak thought philosophy propagated by the Italian postmodern thinkers Gianni Vattimo (b. 1936) and Pier Aldo Rovatti (b. 1942) that advocates the abandonment of an emphasis on objective truth? What is your position on this?

First of all, I would like to stress again the fact that the pope does not say that we should forget or ignore the principles, as some extremists reproach him for. He states that it is necessary to place them in context. On the other hand, a lot of empty words are wasted on the subject of the "weak thought" philosophy! Take heed: the strongest thought is whatever gives us the totality of the Gospel, where different beliefs shine a light on each other and there find their meaning. There is nothing weaker than partial truths that are disconnected and converted into an ideology. In addition, these doctrines become doubly weak if they are not able to convince others. In that case, we end up having to impose them.

On the other hand, the weakest component of our contemporary culture is not what people think, but their habits, their way of life. We know that many people who present themselves as staunch defenders of life have made their wives have abortions, earn money with drug trafficking, are part of some gang through their economic interests, or have supported the war in Iraq. Would all that be representative of strong thought?

Within the Church, there are also many people, including some priests, who have no desire to spend themselves, to serve, to participate in the mission of the Church, who waste much time in discussions, or who are attached to a life full of comforts and pleasures. These are weak practices that can never change the world, for all that they want to stoutly defend certain doctrines. Everything is exactly the opposite with this pope, who, with his teaching and through the example of the dedication of his life, is a strong and immovable rock for the Church and a model for the whole world.

A lively debate has been ignited as a result of a conversation reported in the newspaper La Repubblica *that the pope had on October 1, 2013, with Eugenio Scalfari, a noted journalist and a writer who is a nonbeliever. The following exchange especially has been much discussed: "Your Holiness," Scalfari asks the pope, "you had already written this in the letter that I mentioned. The conscience is autonomous, you said, and everyone must obey their conscience. I think that's one of the most courageous statements made by a pope." Francis replies, "And here I repeat. Each has his or her own idea of good and evil and must choose to follow the good and fight evil as he conceives them. This would be enough to improve the world." Even John Henry Newman spoke of the "primacy of conscience," meaning the same consciousness that "represents God in our hearts." Is this also the case for Francis?*

It is certainly the case; however, this requires an honesty that in today's world is difficult to find. If you told me you were deeply convinced of something, and that after long, deep, and sincere discernment, you really thought that you could not go against that conscience that has developed within you, then you should follow your conscience. However, if you treat everything lightly, according to what you feel like doing, and if you do not listen to others because you are willfully stubborn, if you have not formed your conscience in an honest way, then I would suggest that you should not follow your conscience so readily, because it could generate a lot of suffering for other people. It is one thing to follow one's conscience, and another to follow one's impulses. Today, it is very common to confuse the two.

On the other hand, in *Evangelii Gaudium* the pope reaffirmed the principle of religious freedom, which "includes freedom to 'choose the religion that you consider true'" (EG 255). This presupposes that one is obeying one's conscience, even when it means following a religion that is not Christian. And Pope Francis states this by using a quote from Pope Benedict XVI, which for some reason, has never seriously been taken into consideration.

This is a very specific question. It was John Paul I, Albino Luciani, who called God "Mother." For many theologians, these are the end times in which the Love of God will manifest itself, the Spirit who is above all Mother and listens to everyone without judging. God, in this sense, is a "mother" who wants to welcome us rather than judging us. Do you share this view? Is this the time of God the Mother?

Look, if we go back to the source of the word of God, this thing is as clear as crystal. In the Bible, there is a series of precious texts that speak of the maternal love of God. For example: "Can a woman forget her nursing child, or show no compassion for the child of her womb? Even these may forget, yet I will not forget you. See, I have inscribed you on the palms of my hands" (Isa 49:15–16). And St. Paul speaks about himself at the same time as both a mother (1 Thess 2:7) and a father: "As you know, we dealt with each one of you like a father with his children, urging and encouraging you and pleading that you lead a life worthy of God, who calls you into his own kingdom and glory" (1 Thess 2:11–12). The way in which the pope clearly presents himself is as a father figure to guide and direct, but always with the affection, care, patience, and tenderness of a mother. He is not like a benevolent grandmother that we can lean on, because if she falls, we fall too. Quite the opposite. Millions of people have confidence in him because they see him as loving and respectful, yet at the same time, firm, secure, able to hold the rudder.

A substantial portion of Evangelii Gaudium *is dedicated to homilies. Moreover, a central part of Pope Francis's day is the morning Mass in St. Martha's House, in which the homily has a special significance. Does the large amount of space that the pope dedicated to the homily hold some particular meaning in the overall document or his pastoral plan?*

The pope knows that, in the world of images, the word continues to be very important, but not so much the written word as what is expressed before others. In fact, we remember more things that the pope has said in his sermons than what we read in his documents. The Church transmits its teaching in a special way through preaching because few people actually read the documents. Francis considers the homily to be the characteristic that best distinguishes a good priest from one who is not so good, a priest who knows how to communicate with people from one who cannot make himself understood by the people. He also knows that a botched homily can generate a lot of suffering and keep people away from the Church. This is why he devotes so much space to it.

4

"Coming out of Ourselves"

The Mission to All Parts of the Body

From the Curé of Ars to the priest who people said took on "the smell of the sheep." From the mid-nineteenth-century French priest who, in 2009, was chosen by the Vatican as a model for the contemporary Church, thus arousing controversy among those—including the French Catholic daily *La Croix*—who saw in this "typically Tridentine" figure the entrenchment of an idea of the Church that was antiquated, not to say "medieval," to the model proposed by Jorge Mario Bergoglio, the shepherd who goes down in among the herd and mixes with it so much that he begins to take on the same smell and allows himself to be led rather than lead. This would be enough to explain the reasons behind the undoubted success that Francis has had not only among the people of God, but also in the world beyond it. He manages to reach the hearts of those who are far away, those who have no faith but who see in his putting himself in last place something quite irresistible: the pope who comes down from the throne, the bishop who asks the people to bless him and who drinks some *yerba mate* offered to him by one of the Argentinean faithful on the streets of Rio de Janeiro; the cardinal who, having just put on the white papal vestments, looks out for the first time from the central loggia of the Vatican Basilica and greets the crowd with the words "Good evening" just as St. Francis might have done in the thirteenth century when he roamed through the streets.

It was in late May 2013 when the Italian bishops gathered at the Vatican for their annual general meeting. The pope greeted them one by one in the Basilica of St. Peter. But just a short time before, he had delivered a speech to them in which he spelled out what the bishops must be: not "clerics of state" who were worried only about themselves and their careers, but shepherds, willing to walk "in, among, and behind the flock" and make themselves available to bring the Church "out," even to the peripheries if necessary. There is one concern that the pope has that paradoxically unites him to the first president of the Italian Bishops Conference, Cardinal Giuseppe Siri. During the years of the Cold War, when someone from the left told him he was anticlerical, he replied, "Well, so am I." Meaning that for him, in a similar way as for Siri, the conservative par excellence, anticlericalism was a virtue.

On October 20, 2013, on the occasion of World Mission Sunday, Pope Francis asked the question, "What is the mission of the Church?" His response was, "Spreading the flame of faith throughout the world, which Jesus has ignited in the world: faith in God who is Father, Love, and Mercy." Therefore, he said, "the Christian mission does not mean proselytizing, but sharing that flame that warms the soul." Is proselytizing a danger in the Church today? What is the heart of missionary activity according to Francis?

The mission of the Church has a fundamental objective: that everyone we meet can feel infinitely loved by God beyond their limitations and that they can also regain their dignity and the call to fraternal communion.

However, the pope reminds us that we are not isolated beings and that we live in a culture that often affects us. Evangelizing, he says, tends to transform society and its culture, so that people can grow in an environment that allows them to live in dignity and to feel constantly stimulated to do good. Precisely for this reason, the most important chapter in *Evangelii Gaudium*, which is dedicated to proclaiming the Gospel, deals with the theme of the inculturation of the proclamation and asks us to make a special effort: "The ultimate aim should be that the Gospel, as preached in categories proper to each culture, will create a new synthesis with that particular culture" (EG 129).

The pope uses strong words when he asks us to be more creative in the dialogue between the Gospel and people's culture: "This is always a slow process of which we can be overly fearful. But if we allow doubts and fears to dampen our courage, instead of being creative we will remain comfortable and make no progress whatsoever. In this case we will not take an active part in historical processes, but become mere onlookers as the Church gradually stagnates" (EG 129).

All this has nothing to do with imposing on people or proselytizing, but with a proclamation that "makes their hearts burn within them," and with a sensitivity that encourages us to convey the Gospel through symbols, words, and actions that make them appealing to the sensibilities of others. In India, for example, we have to find words, symbols, and gestures that express the Christian truths in a way that is close to the Indian sensibility. Even within youth culture, we must find symbols that express the beauty of the Gospel to the young. Only in that way will they feel that the Gospel is also addressed to them, that it is relevant to their lives in a tangible way, and that, by doing so, their sense of freedom can open them to listening to the proclamation of the Gospel.

In his first Wednesday general audience, Pope Francis spoke of the need for the Church to come out of itself. He said we must "come out of ourselves…in order to go to meet others, to go toward the

outskirts of existence, to be the first to take a step toward our broth-
ers and our sisters, especially those who are the most distant, those
who are forgotten, those who are most in need of understanding,
comfort and help." Why is it so important to the pope that we as a
Church "come out of ourselves"?

Coming out of oneself is a key to fully understanding what
Pope Francis is thinking and proposing, because the Gospel has a
"drive to go forth and give, to go out from ourselves" (EG 21). It
is the opposite of self-centeredness, which he so deplores.

This is an anthropological, theological, spiritual, and pastoral category that has its roots in the Trinity itself. The three persons are in a mutual and constant relationship, and moreover,
they want a covenant with us. It is from that divine life that the
dynamic movement of coming out of oneself emerges and is
engraved in our hearts through grace. This is the reason why charity, which makes us come out of ourselves toward others, is the
greatest of the virtues. When we say that the Church is missionary
by nature, this is precisely what we are saying: that the Church
was founded in order that it could come out constantly from itself
for service, dialogue, offering, and mission. Metaphysics, which
seeks to explain what is most profound in reality, teaches us that
good itself is widespread, and that whatever is good always tends
to communicate itself. If the reality created by God works in this
way, and if the dynamism of grace is the dynamism of going out,
then the only way to keep ourselves alive is to grow and come out
of ourselves in mission.

If we can understand this, then we stop living on the defensive, we stop being obsessed by our own interests and well-being,
and we discover that the best way to live well is outside of ourselves, seeking the good of all, transmitting good to others, opening ourselves, giving of ourselves.

This also applies to the Christian community. After all, for
the Church, this is a survival strategy, a strategy for being faithful
to itself, to its nature. This means not only keeping a primordial

deposit of doctrines, but above all coming out of itself: to evangelize, to listen, to serve, to transmit life, to remember, and to make present the merciful love of God that drives us forward.

Yet, there seem to be some risks. In particular, the insistence on coming out of ourselves could generate a kind of pastoral activism that becomes an end in itself. Going out could, in a nutshell, make us forget what matters, which is that the origin of every action is none other than Christ himself. Although it is true that we need to come out of ourselves, it is also true that it is important to know where you came from and who it is that you want to bring to the world, to the ends of the earth. So here is the question: Can it not happen that this "coming out of ourselves" becomes mere pastoral activism?

No, not activism, nor is it an attitude only of giving. It is also a receptive attitude. This implies that the Church does not feel like a teacher in the classroom, but rather remains in an attitude that is outward looking, with an openness to the Master. All this for two reasons: because we never stop learning and because the Church itself is neither the owner nor the regulator of the Spirit. The Word embodies a potential that we cannot predict in any way. The Gospel speaks of a seed that, once sown, grows by itself even while the farmer sleeps (cf. Mark 4:26–29). The pope insists that the Church must accept the uncontainable freedom of the Word, which is effective in its own way, and some of its forms, which elude the supervision of the institution of the Church. Accepting all of this is a way for the Church to come out of itself.

This coming out also requires us to dare, to take the first step, not just to sit there hoping for people to come to our meetings or our courses, and to have the courage to talk about Jesus and about our own experience of faith to everyone everywhere. All this happens when the evangelizing community comes to the realization that the Lord has taken the initiative, that he has gone before us in love, and this is how we know how to take the first step toward others, we know how to take the initiative without fear, we know how to go out to meet others, we know how to seek out those who are far away and reach the crossroads where we can invite those who are excluded. We must have an inexhaustible desire to offer mercy, because it is by coming out of ourselves that we receive the infinite mercy of the Father and his strength. The pope always reminds us that the evangelizing community is not closed in on itself but actually shortens the distance to others; we bow down even to the point of humiliation if necessary, taking on responsibility for all of human life and touching the suffering flesh of Christ among the people.

This is not pastoral activism because it can also be expressed in silence. The pope explained that going out to others to reach the outskirts of humanity "does not mean rushing out aimlessly into the world" (EG 46). Often it means to slow down, "to put aside our eagerness in order to see and listen to others, to stop rushing from one thing to another and to remain with someone who has faltered along the way" (EG 46), because sometimes those who rush out into the world remain closed in themselves, in their own needs, in their own obsessions, in their own time. And sometimes, on the other hand, those who come out of themselves are those who disregard their own urgent needs to devote all their attention to another human being. Pope Francis himself behaves like this when, in the midst of a crowd, he stops to listen, to hug someone, to watch.

The pope also met with ecclesial movements in May 2013 and asked them to be missionary. Often movements are criticized for being self-centered, for being like a closed unit that is unable to open up to those who are different from them. These criticisms often come from the people of God themselves, maybe from the parishes, places where the movements struggle to exist. Is this where a new season in the Church must begin, once again primarily among the ecclesial movements that came into existence after Vatican II and that are, as mentioned, often accused of self-centeredness and closedness?

I believe that the grace of ecclesial movements lies in allowing the Church to reach places and sectors of society that it had not reached before or where it is more difficult to reach. They might be close to people who cannot find an answer in the parish structures. Therefore, if they are true to themselves, they should be a valuable channel for the spread of the Gospel and the love of God among those on the margins. Their actions should not focus on finding new people who can enter their movement, but must help people to encounter Jesus, to live with greater dignity, to be happy, to mature, and to become missionaries themselves. Instead, it is a bit annoying at times to listen to some members of the movements speak more about the movement itself, or about its founder, than about Jesus Christ, the love of God, or the Gospel. This is the reason that the pope's invitation to a missionary transformation also benefits the movements.

During the Year for Priests proclaimed by Benedict XVI in 2010, the model of the Curé of Ars was proposed, a priest who waited for people in his church, praying before the Blessed Sacrament. He waited and administered the sacraments, trusting in the power of the Eucharist to attract them. Francis, however, asks everyone, first of all the priests, to go out from their churches and seek people through the streets of the world. What was good about the model of the Curé of Ars? Is he still a figure that should be followed today? And then: Is the Curé of Ars a model for the Church in South America, Africa, and Asia?

The Curé of Ars, especially in the last stage of his life, was able to relate to all the people in his village, and in this sense, we cannot say that he was locked up in his church. However, in all countries, there are examples of missionaries going out to others.

For example, in Argentina, José Gabriel del Rosario Brochero was recently beatified, "the gaucho priest" who set out on horseback and visited all the places hidden in the mountains, looking for the most despised sinners to bring them into the presence of Jesus Christ. Blessed Brochero is also a model of "artisan" or "face-to-face" evangelization that is so dear to this pope, because he was able to converse for hours with an atheist or a great sinner, with patience and courage, as if there were no other person in the world.

In 2007, the Latin American bishops chose Bergoglio as president of the Commission responsible for drafting the final document of the Aparecida Conference. Many felt energized by his evocative language, full of hope, security, and enthusiasm for putting the results into practice. Bergoglio immediately confirmed his commitment to "avoid a self-centered Church" and to work "for a church that would reach all at the peripheries of humanity." It was the beginning of a revolution. For Pope Francis, who are those who are "distant"? What are the peripheries that he asks us to reach?

The "distant" and "peripheries" that we have to reach are not to be understood only in the physical or geographic sense. They can also be found around the corner: those who are not part of the circle of our relationships or our ideological horizon. The problem of some clergymen and certain intellectuals is that they tend to withdraw into small groups and then complain that others are ignorant and do not understand them. The pope's invitation involves opening one's mind, one's group, one's own interests, in order to reach those who are outside or away from one's world. These people can be in the same place of work or in the same neighborhood, physically close but mentally and emotionally distant.

For a Christian community, the peripheries and the distant are those who are not an integral part of the community, and especially those who do not feel included, valued, and loved by the community itself. By using these categories, the pope invites us to overcome the self-centeredness that transforms us into factions, into minorities who resent the fact that we fail to be a leaven of real change because we marginalize ourselves into small restricted groups.

For centuries in the Church, we have had missionaries who leave everything and go off to remote places. The Church has always been missionary, since its beginnings. Who are the missionaries of today? Do the laity also belong to that mission?

Even today we still need many people to find the courage to leave everything and go far away, especially to places where there is great suffering and where the need of Jesus Christ is greater. Nevertheless, most of us are called to be a leaven in the place where we live. We are definitely all missionaries to the extent that we go out looking for those who are distant and on the margins of our own cities, and devote time to them.

Obviously this also applies to the laity, because, as the pope says, "Lay people are, put simply, the vast majority of the people of God. The minority—ordained ministers—are at their service" (EG 102). The whole of the people of God is missionary, and among the people, the ministers represent a small percentage and cannot reach everyone. Laypeople, however, can be found in all environments, and in any context, you can meet a layman who opens new horizons: among businessmen, among fishermen, among rice farmers, wherever it is, everywhere throughout the world. When the pope speaks of the laity, very often he feels the need to clarify this term. We must avoid thinking about laypeople as only those who are part of ecclesial structures or who are close to priests. It would be better to define the laity as the immense multitude of God's people who can ferment the whole world with the leaven of the Gospel. So it makes no sense to ask whether the laity should also be missionaries.

Pope Francis continually calls the faithful to witness. He wants missionaries in the world who are true witnesses of the gospel message. But what is the key to having a heart for the Church's mission in the world?

This question brings us to the last chapter of *Evangelii Gaudium*, which speaks of missionary spirituality. Any mission must have a "spirit" and, for the pope, that means having "an interior impulse which encourages, motivates, nourishes and gives meaning to our individual and communal activity" (EG 261). He explains that evangelization with this spirit is not only accompanied by prayer, but is also fueled by a number of motivations that must always be kept in our hearts. In the last chapter of *Evangelii Gaudium*, he asks us to pause to consider some of these motivations, which are like fuel for a generous offering of ourselves.

The first is "love of Jesus which we have received, the experience of salvation which urges us to ever greater love of him" (EG 264). He writes, "A true missionary, who never ceases to be a disciple, knows that Jesus walks with him, speaks to him, breathes with him, works with him. He senses Jesus alive with him in the midst of the missionary enterprise" (no. 266).

The second is the spiritual realization that we are a people, so that we can "develop a spiritual taste for being close to people's lives and to discover that this is itself a source of greater joy. Mission is at once a passion for Jesus and a passion for his people" (EG 268). In this way, "whenever we encounter another person in love, we learn something new about God. Whenever our eyes are opened to acknowledge the other, we grow in the light of faith and knowledge of God" (no. 272).

The third is the sense of mystery that makes us recognize, behind apparent failures, the mysterious action of the Risen Christ and his Spirit. The resurrection of Jesus "can always pleasantly surprise us. The kingdom is here, it returns, it struggles to flourish anew. Christ's resurrection everywhere calls forth seeds of that new world" (EG 278). Moreover, "there is no greater freedom than that of allowing oneself to be guided by the Holy Spirit, renouncing the attempt to plan and control everything to the last detail, and instead letting him enlighten, guide and direct us, leading us wherever he wills. The Holy Spirit knows well what is needed in every time and place" (no. 280).

Finally, the pope asks us to pray always for others, and that our hearts be deeply intercessory, because it "moves us particularly to take up the task of evangelization and to seek the good of others" (EG 281).

When Bergoglio was Archbishop in Buenos Aires, several pastors took the initiative in facilitating and encouraging in any way they could the celebration of new baptisms. What prompted them, and what prompted Cardinal Bergoglio to encourage this initiative? Sometimes it happens that ministers and pastoral workers assume an attitude that could be called "superior," as if it were in their hands whether to grant the sacraments or not. Should this situation change?

All this has to do with a question of faith, of pure faith, which does not make sense if judged by the standards of what is immediately pastorally efficient. The pope is deeply convinced that taking the initiative by the grace of God is a good thing. In supernatural matters, the first thing is the love of God who is close to us, an infinite love that is beyond compare and cannot be acquired through any human means. Baptizing a child expresses this initiative of God's love in an excellent way: you do not need to pay for it or deserve it. The child did not do anything, but receives it for free, as pure gift. At least, that is something beautiful that is not subject to the laws of the marketplace!

At the same time, baptism sows a spiritual seed in the heart of a child that will remain there, even if the child does not go to Mass or receive a Christian education, even if by the child's words and actions, he or she does not seem Catholic. Nevertheless, that seed will remain within the child, guiding the child toward the good and eventually preparing him or her to die in peace. The Church cannot feel entitled to deny all that to a person. On the contrary, the pope believes that there is need to facilitate it in every possible way and not to impose conditions that complicate or delay receiving the sacrament. It is a free initiative and a gift from God the Father to his creatures out of pure love. This is how it is, and the Church cannot interfere or hinder it but can only facilitate it as an instrument of grace.

All this does not mean, however, that the pope has already made decisions, for example, relating to divorced persons who remarry, because we do not want to send a double message regarding marriage. It is, however, an issue that will be discussed during the next synods, and the pope will listen to the different opinions that will emerge with a distinctly pastoral concern. In *Evangelii Gaudium*, he certainly provided us with an important orientation for our reflection that we cannot fail to take into consideration: he says, "…nor should the doors of the sacraments be closed for simply any reason," and that the Eucharist "is not a prize for the perfect but a powerful medicine and nourishment for the weak" (EG 47). He recommends that we never stop reading the words of St. Ambrose and St. Cyril quoted in note 51, which invite us to not be rigid in the administration of the Eucharist. Neither can we ignore his invitation to be prudent but also to be "daring" in addressing this issue, and his advice to us is not to behave as "arbiters of grace" (no. 47).

It is evident that the sacraments are a central point of every missionary action. According to some, without adequate knowledge and preparation, the sacramental rite risks becoming something magical or even mechanical. What do you think about this?

It is very significant that in *Evangelii Gaudium* there are few references to the sacraments. The element that is most significant is the proclamation of the Gospel. This is understandable, given that it is the central theme of the exhortation. However, all this helps us understand that the sacraments should always be accompanied by proclamation and preaching that help us to understand them more deeply. So, in the thinking of this pope, the emphasis should not be placed so much on doctrinal instruction as on helping the faithful to discover the profound spirit of the sacrament.

However, we must remember the great value that the pope attaches to having compassion for the poor and the simple who have not received doctrinal formation, but express their faith in other ways. He does not think that the community of the faithful has a magical or mechanical attitude. For example, even when the poor touch the image of Mary, they do it with a deep trust in their hearts, and at times, those who are more educated do so with little enthusiasm, because they have more confidence in their own ideas or their own ability than in what the Lord can accomplish. In Catholic countries, the poor in general feel a deep affection toward baptism, and although they are not able to explain the doctrine about it, they believe very strongly that what happens during baptism is very important, and it is therefore necessary for their children to be baptized.

In *Evangelii Gaudium*, the pope mentions the distinction between the knowledge of faith and adherence to it and writes that "some things are understood and appreciated only from the standpoint of this assent, which is a sister to love, beyond the range of clear reasons and arguments" (EG 42). For this reason, sacramental preparation should be geared mainly to this.

Does the fact that Pope Francis insists so much on the first ardent proclamation of the Gospel mean that he places less importance on the need for formation?

No, that's not the way he means it. What is close to the Holy Father's heart is that people grow, mature, and deepen their faith.

However, experience teaches us that we must fully understand the meaning of our formation. There are people who have done many courses, read a lot, know a lot about doctrine, but that does not mean that they are able to live their faith with joy, or that they are more generous or consistent. Cardinal Bergoglio was aware of this and spoke about it often. So now he emphasizes catechesis that focuses more on the central proclamation of faith, on what is most important, most beautiful and attractive, because it is the personal experience of the encounter with a God who loves and frees us and calls us to fellowship that ensures that a person will want to offer to God a life that is consistent, dedicated, and generous.

In this sense, the Holy Father is much more interested in how people believe joyfully and deeply, rather than that they have detailed knowledge of a multitude of doctrines and religious information. This is not to say that it is not important to grow in the knowledge of the whole of Catholic doctrine, but the biggest risk lies in not being happily aware of the most beautiful and the greatest elements in the Gospel. We must always come back to this catechesis; focused on the proclamation, says the pope, try to live it fully, and not forget about it because of our encyclopedic religious formation. What the pope says in this document regarding catechesis is something very demanding and revolutionary and will ruffle the feathers of people and facilities who adopt it. They will need to thoroughly revise their plans, programs, and manuals of catechesis.

Is it true that Pope Francis does not show much enthusiasm for the contributions of intellectuals?

No. There is no way we can say that he devalues reflection or study. He himself has devoted many hours to reading and studying different issues and has always had the pleasure of conversing with educated people: philosophers, writers, artists, researchers from the different sciences. In *Evangelii Gaudium*, he repeats an expression from *Dei Verbum* that emphasized how the work of exegetes is an aid for "maturing the judgment of the Church," but he also extends this to theologians and states that "the other sciences also help to accomplish this, each in its own way" (EG 40). Also, he refers to the "great freedom" of thought and research that must be present in the Church (no. 40), and recalls that "universities are outstanding environments for articulating and developing this evangelizing commitment in an interdisciplinary and integrated way" (no. 134). He is interested in the Church deepening its thought and its knowledge of the whole of reality. Contrary to what some would have us think, taking up the call to mission does not make us brainless!

It is also true, however, that the pope never tires of asking theologians not to be "content with a desk-bound theology," but to live "as part of the Church's saving mission" (EG 133). In this sense, what most annoys him are some people who use incomprehensible language and end up not contributing to anything, simply because no one understands them. What is good must be communicated, so even intellectuals are called to make an effort to be humble so that their contributions can reach others. Francis has observed that if intellectuals are vain, then they demonstrate that they possess only information and not wisdom.

5

Reform within the Church

The Structures and Privileges

From the beginning of his pontificate, Pope Francis has hinted that he wants to reform the Church, keeping what is good and purifying what is not going well. Rather than a reform of structures, from the Roman Curia to the various ecclesial bodies scattered around the world—however necessary a reform of these may be—the pope has suggested that his idea of renewal is primarily spiritual. It is key that every believer is called to convert to Christ, so that the whole Church, bit by bit, becomes more and more conformed to his person, his true message.

Although the Church is not formed predominantly by priests, it is to them that Francis has directed his most important exhortations and sometimes even the harshest warnings, so that they will be true ministers of God and not men devoted to careerism or privileges.

On May 15, 2013, during a homily at St. Martha's House, Pope Francis said, "When a priest or a bishop goes after money, the people do not love him and that's a sign. But he himself ends up badly...." And again, speaking of St. Paul: "He did not have a bank account; he worked." And then, even more harsh words: "And when a bishop or a priest is on the road to vanity, he enters into the spirit of careerism, and it hurts the Church so much that in the end he becomes ridiculous, he likes to boast, he likes to show off, he acts as if he is all powerful....And people do not like that!" The two temptations from which bishops and priests must guard are "wealth" and "vanity."

It was not the first time that Bergoglio has denounced careerism, "spiritual worldliness," as the biggest danger in the Church. His reform is based on continually calling us back to have an evangelical spirit: "In the last analysis a bishop is not a bishop for himself, he is for the people; and a priest is not a priest for himself, he is for the people." He said again in his May 15 homily that the proper service of the shepherd is "protecting his flock from wolves. When the bishop does so, he creates a good relationship with the people, like Paul the bishop had with his people: there is a love between them, a real love, and the Church becomes united." Because a reform of the Church will come, what is needed are people who know how to avoid those temptations of which St. Augustine wrote: "Wealth, which can become greed, and vanity." When a bishop or a priest "takes advantage of the sheep for himself, the dynamic changes: it is not the priest or the bishop, for the people—but the priest and the bishop who take from the people." The author of the *Confessions*, recalled the pope, says that whoever "takes the meat from the sheep to eat, takes advantage; he makes deals and is attached to money; he becomes greedy and even sometimes practices simony. Perhaps he takes advantage of the wool for vanity, in order to vaunt himself."

Fr. Víctor, there is much talk in Rome about the reform of the structure of the Church: a new Roman Curia, first of all. They say that the true reform of the Church is not in the structures but in everyone's heart. What do you think Bergoglio's idea of reform is?

The two things, the inner life and external reform, proceed together and simultaneously. Francis's idea of reform is not an ideal but something concrete. No doubt he thinks that a reform of the external structures is not sustainable without a spirit and an appropriate way of life. Without mincing words, he states that "good structures are only helpful when there is a life constantly driving, sustaining and assessing them. Without new life and an authentic evangelical spirit, without the Church's 'fidelity to her own calling,' any new structure will soon prove ineffective" (EG 26).

It seems to me that the most important thing about this is not the simplification of the structures of the Roman Curia so much as the development of alternative forms of participation (such as synods, bishops' conferences, and consultations with the laity) that in recent years have been more cosmetic than real. Undoubtedly, such progress implies that certain sectors of the Roman Curia will have to abandon certain overly inquisitive and magisterial attitudes that run the risk of becoming self-centered. Sometimes I have heard some people in the Curia use the word *we* in reference to themselves, excluding the whole Church and even the pope. Francis reminds us that Jesus gave a special mission to Peter and the apostles. He did not bestow it on a central structure that can do nothing but play an auxiliary role of service.

However, I don't think that we should focus so much on the reform of the Roman Curia. It is not a subject that anyone is going to lose sleep over, as they say. This reform is necessary from a point of view that we can define as "negative": that is, in order to avoid excessive centralization, not stifle dialogue and local initiatives, and not impose suffocating control. From the point of view of morality and witness, financial-level reforms are also very important. But the reform of the Church goes infinitely further than all that, because its purpose is to allow the Church, around the world, to become a better instrument for the transmission of good, the spread of the light of the Gospel, creating a civilization of love, the communication of God's love which saves, heals, unites, and ennobles. To accomplish this mission, the Church needs to be transformed into a place of lively participation where all persons are active subjects, thanks to the richness of their charisms. I believe that true reform should proceed in that direction.

There is much talk, as I said, about the reform of the Roman Curia, but much less about the general reform of the governance of the Church. What does Pope Francis have in mind for this? The convening, in Rome, of a council of eight cardinals from every continent to help him suggests the desire to achieve real collegial governance within the Church in the wake of the wishes expressed in the first place by the Second Vatican Council. Is that so? What kind of collegiality does Francis intend to implement?

Francis himself has taken on the collegiality of the Orthodox Churches. He has said that we have much to learn from their experience. He has taken up again and emphasized the invitation by John Paul II to think about the exercise of the papacy in a different way, a way that favors communion. It is apparent, therefore, that he wants to convert the Church into a place of lively and vibrant participation, a place where ideas can be exchanged free from fear, a place of amiable and sincere conversation, a place of listening, where everyone can express themselves and be taken into consideration. In this sense, the Council of eight cardinals should not be made absolute, because turning it into an oligarchy would not be a good thing. The eight cardinals cannot even think about coming together to represent all the lines of thought and all the concerns that are present in the Church.

The word *collegiality* is the one that best expresses the goal. It implies the presence of mechanisms by which the whole Church can feel represented and heard. It presupposes that more autonomy be given to local churches and that they talk to each other, so that they can build that "polyhedron" that the pope has in mind. On this point, the pope immediately recognized that the Synod of Bishops, in the way it was operating, was not fulfilling its role, because, in the only meetings that were organized, the bishops could not express themselves freely and the discussions were too limited and conditioned by the Roman Curia.

A topic that repeatedly comes up when talking about the reform of the Church is the role of the episcopal conferences. With Francis at the helm, what will happen to the Episcopal Conferences throughout the world? Sometimes they are huge structures, a kind of bureaucracy sitting above the faithful, which is hardly perceived as a service structure.

Your question reminds me of something that I had not thought of. In my personal experience, I have never really considered that in other places, the situation might be different, such as in Italy. Episcopal conferences need more freedom of opinion and response to local challenges; therefore, decentralization is required in order to avoid excessive control by the Roman Curia. This does not mean that we create a gigantic structure in each country that transforms the bishops' conference itself into a new and top-heavy Roman Curia.

Saying that the conferences should have more autonomy means that they need a space in which local problems are discussed and reflected on and where appropriate solutions can be found to the challenges of that place. For this to happen, the bishops should let there be more freedom and allow other people to participate, so that the conference is not a huge, heavy structure, but rather the opposite: a channel for dialogue, expression, and participation. This is the pope's idea, since he is against big structures that exist solely for the purpose of sustaining themselves. He rejects the excess of organization that leads us to lose too much time in controls, schedules, evaluations, and endless discussion because what matters is closeness to the people, the ability to empathically understand their problems, and face-to-face evangelization. Too many superfluous structures, however useful, end up crushing this dynamism and mean that we expend all our energy in a self-referential mechanism. Pope Francis has made it clear that reform only makes sense if it is done with a missionary goal. Otherwise, any reform would be a deception and would simply turn some structures into heavier ones.

Journalists who cover events occurring in the Church are like sensors that pick up sound waves. These waves are of various types, not all positive, some even negative. Sometimes, for example, you come across bishops (these are a minority, but they do exist) who, as soon as they have been appointed to one diocese, start agitating to leave, looking for promotions to what they see as the most prestigious venues. And they talk about it openly, as if it were completely normal. Of course, there are many godly pastors in the world, but some are also careerists. Is it possible that, in the future, a practice will be adopted whereby a bishop assigned to a diocese remains there for a lifetime? What solutions can be found to the problem of careerism?

It is easier to be a careerist if there is a great deal of centralization. All you need to do is flatter those in power, repeat what they say, and give them gifts. But it is much more difficult when you are in the presence of wider community discernment, when those around you have to assess your skills and your attitudes. It is easier to fool your boss than your colleagues, and to fool your superior rather than the community. In this sense, too, decentralization is very important and so is achieving the increased participation that this pope is talking about.

Another wound the Church has suffered much from is the sin of the clergy. In the year 2010, the international media published details of several cases of child abuse committed by priests. Some allegations were not true, but others were. Pope Benedict XVI has done a lot not only for transparency, but also for eradicating a heinous

crime that, because it is perpetrated by priests, creates dismay, bewil-
derment, and anger. How does Francis want to proceed with this?

I think we have made progress in facilitating our procedures, particularly in preventing those who have been the perpe-
trators of this deplorable behavior, or who have been the subject
of repeated and credible allegations, from doing further harm to
others. Certainly, it is necessary that all this should be carried out
in a prudent and responsible way, so that we do not irreparably
ruin the reputation of innocent people or give rise to vendettas,
threats, or extortion: unfortunately this has happened too.

But we must ask forgiveness, especially for cases in which
this crime was easily demonstrable and decisions were not made
promptly. All this makes us ashamed, and we believe that, in
those situations, it was clear that the biggest risk was the fact that
such sick people could continue to harm the children. Today,
the orientation of the Church is very clear and guidelines are
adequate. Surely, the pope had all this in mind when he spoke of
"the pain and the shame we feel at the sins of some members of
the Church" (EG 76).

There is another sensitive issue. It is a fact that many married people are also pedophiles. However, for all we try to explain
it, society does not believe it. There is a general belief that mandatory celibacy and the priestly environment formed only by men
facilitate not only the development of homosexual inclinations
but also abuse. Therefore, even if this reasoning does not convince us, I think we should listen more to the people of God and,
as far as possible, open a serious debate on mandatory celibacy.
Regardless of the conclusions that may emerge, the mere fact of
opening it up would be a very positive sign. But this is just a personal opinion.

In European Catholicism especially, which is closer to the Prot-
estant world, people, not only the lay faithful but also priests and

bishops, regularly call for the abolition of compulsory priestly celibacy. In fact, celibacy is not a dogma, but a law. And as such, it may well be abolished. Will Francis push for reforms in this area?

In reality, I think that custom seems to have more weight than conviction, because celibacy is not inseparable from the priesthood, and there are Catholic priests in the East who are happily married. With regard to all that, however, the pope has said some things, very interesting but also destabilizing, that are worth remembering: "In her ongoing discernment, the Church can also come to see that certain customs not directly connected to the heart of the Gospel, even some which have deep historical roots, are no longer properly understood and appreciated. Some of these customs may be beautiful, but they no longer serve as means of communicating the Gospel. We should not be afraid to re-examine them" (EG 43).

We must clarify, however, that this does not mean that we call into question the value of celibacy, which continues to be a wonderful sign that many priests live with great spiritual fruitfulness. What is being discussed here is only whether it should still be obligatory. It is clear that it is not essential. There are married Eastern priests whose priesthood does not have less value because of the fact that they are married, and whose marriage is not a "permitted sin." We must, therefore, ask whether the reasons for accepting married priests in the East are not of value even today for the West.

Let's talk about women priests. The Protestant world in part allows them. Why does the Catholic Church not have this option? Pope Francis, on the occasion of the twenty-fifth anniversary of Mulieris Dignitatem, *said that he suffers when he sees women having a role of servitude in the Church. What role does the pope see for women? What role can better show that women are valued in the Church today?*

God made sure that only women could bear children, but we don't rebel against that. Why is there a problem with conferring the priesthood only on men?

I sincerely believe that this happens because the priesthood is too often identified with power in the Church; that is why many cannot accept that only men can hold this office. The fact that Jesus Christ has reserved the priesthood for men has to do with the symbolic meaning of the priesthood. During the Mass, the priest represents Christ who offers himself to his bride, the church community. The figure of the man is more suitable in this regard. However, there is no reason to restrict authority, the leadership of the community, access to the functions of power, and decision-making to men only. This is the point over which we need to fully deepen our understanding.

Traditionally, it is said that the priest is a sign of Christ "the Head." In reality, this expression was intimately related to grace "from the head," which is the grace that descends from Christ the Head of the body that is the Church, especially in the Eucharist. So, we are referring mainly to the priest who, as minister of the Eucharist, becomes an instrument of the action of Jesus Christ for the good of his Church. Sometimes the term *head* is, however, associated with domination, power, and authority, and that is why a theology of the priesthood has developed that identifies priests too much with power. We can understand, then, why it is difficult to accept that only men have access to it. But the pope has taken a clear stand against this view, stating that the identification of the priest with Christ the Head "does not imply an exaltation which would set him above others," and that "its key and axis is not power understood as domination." Moreover, he stresses that this has important consequences for "the possible role of women in decision-making" (EG 104). At the beginning of the same paragraph, he notes that the fact that men and women have the same dignity presents the Church with "profound and challenging questions which cannot be lightly evaded." So the pope's proposal is to separate the priesthood from the power, so as to remove conflict over the subject of the male priesthood.

In the interview with La Civiltà Cattolica, *Bergoglio cites the Jesuit Blessed Peter Favre as his model, and he also speaks of him in Evangelii Gaudium. Is he holding him up as an example for the whole Church, as a missionary and a witness of Christ in the world? Who was Favre? Why does Bergoglio refer to him with such consistency, to the point of wanting to accelerate the canonization process?**

This holy Jesuit, one of the first companions of St. Ignatius, was a master of gentleness, patience, and dialogue with everyone. Bergoglio remembers a sentence of Favre's where he says that "time is the messenger of God," and he sums it up with his principle: "time is greater than space." Favre preferred not to waste time in theoretical discussions with Protestants and stressed the need for the Church to mature and grow as a witness to the Gospel. I think this has a lot to do with Pope Francis, who distances himself from theoretical disputes and is able to express his beliefs through a very attractive testimony. Reforms cannot be carried out by force or in a hurry because they must always be accompanied by spiritual growth, and that takes some time. All this is clearly present in Favre's, as well as in Pope Francis's style.

In what way will this missionary transformation that the pope proposes modify the style and structure of parishes?

For Pope Francis, in reforming the parish, it is essential that it "really is in contact with the homes and the lives of its people, and does not become a useless structure out of touch with people" (EG 28). Often, there are institutions that are organized on a large scale, but the people you are targeting cannot find anyone

---

*Pope Francis declared Pierre Favre a saint on December 17, 2013.

willing to listen and to help. Other times, however, these institutions are not popular because people cannot identify with them and do not feel as though they are their own. All this would be tragic for a parish. On the other hand, some pastors devote much time to the organization of courses and meetings but little time to assisting their faithful and, when they do, it is always with the same people, who will never change into evangelizers of society.

This is why the pope proposes the idea of a "missionary option, that is, a missionary impulse capable of transforming everything, so that the Church's customs, ways of doing things, times and schedules, language and structures can be suitably channeled for the evangelization of today's world rather than for her self-preservation" (EG 27). Reforming the structures that are required for that pastoral conversion has a single aim: to allow them to become more missionary, more expansive and open, and to place pastoral workers in a constant attitude of going out. However, it must be a going out that results in nearness and contact. Pope Francis is in love with all that is "homemade" and face-to-face, with a plan that is rolled out slowly and laboriously. He has never liked congresses and meetings that dwell on what should have been done or, even less, on what others would have to do. Therefore, in Buenos Aires, what bothered him were the parishes that made a show of having great organization but paid no attention to the people, did not go through the streets or visit their neighbors' homes.

Nor is he attracted to those who engage in endless discussions but never generate new initiatives that could be useful for going forward. He considers those who sit in judgment without lifting a finger to help to be the worst enemies of good projects and dreams. His personal example shows us another way and shows us that we have been asleep, closed, and that we had reached an impasse that kept us away from the people.

This was happening both among the people on the "right" and among those on the "left." In countries like Brazil, for example, many priests focused all their energy on meetings in which they spoke of the poor, while the poor themselves, because of lack of spiritual attention, ended up by turning to the evangelical communities. In other places, the priests' meetings focused on bioethics, but the consequences were similar.

Within the Church, in the first months of his pontificate, there was some criticism of the pope. Many, as stated, were conservatives and were always reluctant to undertake any form of renewal. Some have even called it ironic that this pope, who comes under intense scrutiny and enjoys widespread support throughout the whole world, is simultaneously concerned with the reform of the papacy and the decentralization of the Church.

I believe that it is precisely his ability to detach himself from centralized power that is a further sign of his humility and his honesty, and all this makes him a credible figure. In addition to that, it should also be taken into account that several paragraphs of *Evangelii Gaudium* reveal his desire to demystify the papacy and ask for help from other people's charisms. He emphasizes this point a lot, and it is worth rereading what he says:

> Nor do I believe that the papal magisterium should be expected to offer a definitive or complete word on every question which affects the Church and the world. It is not advisable for the Pope to take the place of local Bishops. (EG 16)

> It is not the task of the Pope to offer a detailed and complete analysis of contemporary reality, but I do exhort all the communities. (no. 51)

> Neither the Pope nor the Church have a monopoly on the interpretation of social realities or the proposal of solutions to contemporary problems. (no. 184)

We already have valuable texts of the magisterium and celebrated writings by great authors. I do not claim to replace or improve upon these treasures. (no. 260)

In addition, in other paragraphs, he refers to the need for the Church to seek help from other sciences (EG 40, 133, 182), and he even says that "whenever the sciences—rigorously focused on their specific field of inquiry—arrive at a conclusion which reason cannot refute, faith does not contradict it" (no. 243). This is not inconsistent with the specific charism of the pope or with the special assistance given to him by the Spirit. However, he is so realistic, humble, and honest!

6

In What Sense Are We a People?

Pope Francis has repeatedly revived the image of the "people of God" in its widest sense, that is, enlarged, not closed in on itself. This image was already fully covered by Vatican II, but too many, in the period after the Council, have wanted to negate it. The Church, from Bergoglio's perspective, is not a set of isolated individuals, but rather a community that includes laypeople of all ages, from the young people that Francis met in Brazil to the elderly, such as his grandmother Rosa, whom he has often quoted. This image is also associated with the rejection of the concept of the Church as a small chapel that contains only a select few. The Church is not just for the elite: the hierarchy and the pope himself should enter into dialogue with the people of God. All are equally welcome, not just expert theologians or the clergy.

In short, the "people of God" as intended by Pope Francis is the same "people of God" that the Council spoke about, particularly in the Dogmatic Constitution *Lumen Gentium*, which covers the topic of the people before turning to the hierarchy. This is no coincidence. The *Catechism of the Catholic Church* acknowledges the renewal of the Council and devotes a discussion to "The Church—People of God." This is how the Catechism describes the characteristics of the people of God (no. 782):

—God is not the property of any one people. But he acquired a people for himself from those who previously were not a people: "a chosen race, a royal priesthood, a holy nation" (1 Pet 2:9).

—One becomes a *member* of this people not by a physical birth, but by being "born anew," a birth "of water and the Spirit" (Jn 3:3–5), that is, by faith in Christ, and Baptism.

—This People has for its Head Jesus the Christ (the anointed, the Messiah). Because the same anointing, the Holy Spirit, flows from the head into the body, this is "the messianic people."

—"The *status* of this people is that of the dignity and freedom of the sons of God, in whose hearts the Holy Spirit dwells as in a temple."

—"Its *law* is the new commandment to love as Christ loved us" (cf. Jn 13:34). This is the "new" law of the Holy Spirit (Rom 8:2; Gal 5:25).

—Its *mission* is to be salt of the earth and light of the world (cf. Mt 5:13–16). This people is "a most sure seed of unity, hope, and salvation for the whole human race."

—Its *destiny*, finally, "is the Kingdom of God which has been begun by God himself on earth and which must be further extended until it has been brought to perfection by him at the end of time" (LG 9 § 2; cf. no. 36).

———

In Argentina, some Catholics have coined the expression "from inhabitants to citizens." It is said about Bergoglio, sotto voce, that he has corrected this expression, arguing that we should also say, "From citizens to a people." What did he mean by this phrase? Why this emphasis?

THE FRANCIS PROJECT

This is an important issue in the thought of Pope Francis, and we must not take it lightly. It is true that the history of Europe in the twentieth century led to a rejection of the category of "people" because of its links with totalitarian regimes. Even in this age, certain political currents cause disgust when, guided by their thirst for power, they speak of the people only in order to manipulate it and to exploit its weaknesses and needs. None of this is part of the notion of a people used by the pope, which is in fact profoundly beautiful. He explains that "people in every nation enhance the social dimension of their lives by acting as committed and responsible citizens, not as a mob swayed by the powers that be" (EG 220). It is precisely on this point that he highlights to us the difference between a simple collection of citizens and a people.

On the one hand, Francis cites a passage from the bishops of the United States: "Being a faithful citizen is a virtue, and participation in political life is a moral obligation." Here, he recognizes that there is a need to stop being merely inhabitants of a territory who think only like consumers, and instead, we must become citizens who are responsible, honest, and who have ethical beliefs and are respectful of the institutions. However, all this is not enough. And so he invites us to go a step further, saying that "becoming a people demands something more. It is an ongoing process in which every new generation must take part: a slow and arduous effort calling for a desire for integration and a willingness to achieve this through the growth of a peaceful and multifaceted culture of encounter" (EG 220). To become a people means being able to reach agreements that would constitute a common project into which everyone can be integrated in some way, where the poor are not excluded, where there are no outcasts, where there are no second-class citizens. If we claim to build a society based solely on our way of thinking—on the criteria and the cultural style of a few enlightened ones who feel superior to all the rest—while others should learn from them and become citizens according to their edicts, there will never be a people.

In What Sense Are We a People?

As we have said, the whole of the second chapter of the Dogmatic Constitution on the Church, Lumen Gentium, *is dedicated to the "people of God." That conciliar text speaks about the people before going on to speak about the hierarchy. Why is that?*

Because it is vital that ministers rediscover that they too are, first of all, part of the people of God, within the people and not above it. In *Evangelii Gaudium*, however, we speak of God's people as the whole of the baptized, without any reference to the hierarchy. The members of the hierarchy are usually very aware of their belonging to the Church, but the pope wants all the baptized, without exception, to understand that they too are, by right, part of the missionary Church.

In this pope's thinking, the idea of being a people suggests that the authorities are at the service of others without ceasing to be part of their lives and of their pilgrimage. Let us remember that some are very helpful and generous but with a touch of vanity that makes them feel more important than others.

Authority is necessary because of the bond of communion and service for the care of the common good that prevents anyone from attacking that good, which is for everyone, for their own personal gain. However, this does not mean that there should be privileges, adulation, better economic status, or luxury; there should not be ill-treatment or persecution of those who think differently, or even attempts at proselytizing that do not respect the freedom of others. Whoever has authority, both within the Church and in other areas, must humbly accept criticism and complaints and accept that service is a sacrifice. For this reason, Pope Francis does not tolerate people within the Church who are obsessed with recognition or privileges. Anyone who receives a ministry in the Church must never stop being part of the people, and becoming part of the people means living among people, humbly at their service in the ordained ministry. They can call others to obedience when necessary, but without pretensions to glory or favorable treatment. Francis explains it very well in *Evangelii Gaudium* when he calls those who evangelize to offer themselves generously: "Jesus does not want us to be grandees who look down upon others, but men and women of the people....We achieve fulfillment when we break down walls and our heart is filled with faces and names! (EG 271, 274).

In theology, what does it mean to be the people of God?

For a time, the Church was considered to be a structured society and, above all, a hierarchical structure; the external and legal aspect was accentuated. At other times, it was understood in a particular spiritual way, such as a mystical body, animated by the Holy Spirit. The category of people of God is more inclusive and integral, because it focuses on people in their relation to each other, who are walking together at a certain point in history animated by the Spirit. This is expressed in the words "she is certainly a mystery rooted in the Trinity, yet she exists concretely in history as a people of pilgrims and evangelizers, transcending any institutional expression, however necessary" (EG 111). God calls us "as a people and not as isolated individuals...God attracts us by taking into account the complex interweaving of personal relationships entailed in the life of a human community" (EG 113).

This notion of the people of God includes everyone, laypeople and ministers, parishes and movements, all with their own charisms. It includes the life of grace, which acts beyond what is visible, and includes the Supreme Pastor who guides us, who is Jesus, but also the pope and all the ministers who assist him. It also includes the Church's relationship with the world and, specifically, with all the peoples of the earth; it includes the path and the history that we are building together in our pilgrimage on this earth. Moreover, it has an eschatological dimension: in heaven, we will not come across structures and authorities or the sacraments, but, having reached the end of our pilgrimage, we will remain the people of God with an immense wealth of relationships that have been healed and made beautiful through the life of the Trinity.

Why are some so critical of the famous "theology of the people" in Argentina, which Bergoglio also shares? Do these criticisms come from conservatives?

Not necessarily. The theology of the people is different from either the Marxist view or the liberal vision. For this reason, neither of the two points of view is enamored by it and they consider it to be a kind of populism. When it comes to the attack on the theology of the people, Marxists and right-wing liberals are in agreement, which indicates that they persist in theoretical "desk-bound" positions that are distant from the people. A friend of mine used to say that if some Western Marxists dared to meet a worker, they would faint because they have never seen one before. So the pope insists that "reality is greater than ideas," and that conceptual formulations do not always express reality, which escapes us and goes beyond our theories.

It is usually said that the theology of the people loves the ignorant masses, who are devoid of culture and critical thinking. What the theology of the people defends is quite different. It means considering the poor not so much simply as the object of liberation or instruction, but rather as individuals who are able to think according to their lights, are capable of legitimately living the faith in their own way, and are able to create pathways out of their own popular culture. The fact that they think, express themselves, or look at life in a different way does not mean they do not think or do not have a culture; it is simply a different culture, different from that of the middle class. The term *people* is distinguished from the word *masses* because it assumes a collective capable of generating its own historical processes. You can contribute something, you can allow the poor to progress toward the path of education and maturity, but you can also help them to develop in the best way that God has given them, respecting their identity and their way of life.

There are areas in society and in the Church that are very class conscious. They feel they belong to a special group of people who have good formation, are enlightened, and are guardians of the truth. They constantly repeat a set of slogans from this untouchable mindset, and because of that, they believe they are the masters of an uneducated and mindless mass of people who should simply follow the guidelines handed down to them from this elite class from their ivory tower. These kinds of people, whether they are from the right or the left, find it impossible to believe that the poor possess their own wisdom, their own truth, and their own capacity for considered opinion.

Many, however, have called this theology "progressive." Is this wrong, in your opinion? And if so, why?

I do not think the word *progressive* is the most appropriate for interpreting the thoughts of Francis. In general, the "greats" are difficult to classify because they transcend the patterns that we use to interpret reality. This pope is a man who has always boldly encouraged innovation, change, and new departures, but these can never be created out of nothing, in a vacuum. On the contrary, he knows that history is fertile ground, a rich compost full of vitality that we must continually take advantage of. He himself says, "Nor should we see the newness of this mission as entailing a kind of displacement or forgetfulness of the living history which surrounds us and carries us forward" (EG 13). Pure progressivism runs the risk of finding itself without roots, and therefore dried out. It is another thing, however, to change and grow, allowing the best new ideas to grow, beginning with what one has received from those who have gone before us and from the long history behind us. This is Francis's style.

In What Sense Are We a People?

On the other hand, when it comes to theology of the people, one might wonder what is more progressive, getting close to the people from above, feeling that we are wise saviors of a despicable rabble who are without conscience, or doing so from the inside, treating the children of this people as valuable individuals capable of generating a distinct culture, despite our help, despite what we offer them in the way of formation and organization.

What part does popular piety play in all of this?

Popular piety is the way most Catholics live out their faith. It is people's experience of faith that finds a legitimate expression in their own culture, in their lifestyle. It represents the inculturated spirituality of the Gospel, which has fertilized popular culture. In the life of the people, popular piety is not spirituality for the masses, nor is it simply the sum of their collective acts. It would be only a poor caricature of popular piety if we presented a contemptuous vision that tries to reduce it to a few mechanical acts by an impersonal crowd of people who do not understand the meaning of what they are doing. While it is true that popular piety is expressed through pilgrimages and communal acts, that is not the whole story; it also finds expression in the daily life of the individuals who make up the people. The *Aparecida Document* states that "popular piety delicately permeates the personal existence of each believer, and even though he or she lives in a multitude, it is not a 'mass spirituality.' At different moments of daily struggle, many go back to some small sign of God's love" (AD 261). It also shows that people who take part in a pilgrimage experience something very "personal," because, for example, "the pilgrim's gaze rests on an image that symbolizes God's affection and closeness. Love pauses, contemplates mystery, and enjoys it in silence....A living spiritual experience is compressed into a brief moment" (no. 259).

This popular piety has a lot to do with the cultural dimension of all the people in whom the Church lives and works, because the people of God "is incarnate in the peoples of the earth, each of which has its own culture" (EG 115). However, it is transmitted through many symbols and gestures, because "in their process of transmitting their culture they also transmit the faith in ever new forms" (EG 122). And the pope adds this exhortation: "Let us not stifle or presume to control this missionary power!" (EG 124).

What, strictly speaking, is pastoral care?

It is missionary renewal that is truly broad, generous, and incisive, that summons all and must gather the people together as its focus. In other words, this renewal does not come into being thanks to a handful of selected pastoral agents who go out to the majority of people who would be on the other side to receive them. Each of the baptized faithful, whatever his or her degree of faith, is an agent of evangelization, "a missionary disciple." Certainly, we are all called to grow as evangelizers, offering more training, a deepening of our love, and a clearer witness to the Gospel. However, that does not mean postponing or deferring our mission of evangelization to some future date, but rather helping others so that all may find a way to communicate the fact that Jesus is the answer in every situation in which they find themselves. Neither imperfection nor sin is an excuse. All that is required is simply to bear witness to one's experience of being imperfect and limited, but happy to be saved and with a strong desire to grow again.

Of course, it is still necessary to build real pastoral care. Cardinal Bergoglio always spoke of this urgent task because some oversimplify the meaning of pastoral care, which is something much more revolutionary than what we normally think.

Offering people devotions or forms of piety is fine but is not strictly part of a pastoral care. Pastoral care assumes that initiatives emerge that have been put forward by the leaders among the people, people who do not conform to our mental and ecclesial structures or to our culture, but who have strong faith, leadership qualities, and an attractiveness that comes from the Spirit. By developing this ministry, we can make progress in the inculturation of the Gospel in those areas, although it requires courage, trust in the Spirit and in the people among whom we work, and an ability to break free from the need to keep everything under control and restrict pastoral care to the confines of our own plans.

Precisely because it can reach everyone, the Holy Spirit also enriches the whole Church with charisms of all kinds as it evangelizes. The charisms are not assets that are restricted and handed over to one group to care for. But rather from these charisms grow special abilities and emphases, initiatives that are sometimes strange and perhaps even annoying, which are, however, able to reach areas among the people that no one else can reach. For this reason, they should be not so much tolerated as welcomed within the body of the Church. For certain, the Spirit is distributing all the new charisms necessary to reach every person at this point in history and through the culture in which each person operates. However, we have to help people to recognize these charisms and bring them to fruition without fear. Otherwise our message will reach very few people. In any case, what should be jealously protected is the integration of the different charisms and of people's various abilities into the whole, so that we do not damage communion among ourselves.

We know that for Bergoglio, the notion of being a people is linked to a broader idea of culture, which allows us to go beyond individuality and thus think of more widespread evangelization. However, I understand that you are speaking about an inculturation of the Gospel, which, in some ways, is a product of the Christian tradition. Could you explain how this can be useful to those who are called to evangelize in some Asian countries in which, for example, the culture does not bear the characteristics of intense evangelization?

In those countries, the effort to evangelize the culture and the inculturation of the Gospel may seem utopian, but it is undoubtedly a real goal that distinguishes a certain pastoral style. The pope is aware of the difficulties that you mentioned, and that is why it is expressed well in this important passage: "In countries where Christianity is a minority, then, along with encouraging each of the baptized to proclaim the Gospel, particular Churches should actively promote at least preliminary forms of inculturation. The ultimate aim should be that the Gospel, as preached in categories proper to each culture, will create a new synthesis with that particular culture. This is always a slow process of which we can be overly fearful. But if we allow doubts and fears to dampen our courage, instead of being creative, we will remain comfortable and make no progress whatsoever. In this case we will not take an active part in historical processes, but become mere onlookers as the Church gradually stagnates" (EG 129).

In reality, it is a dynamism that you must feed through things that are simple and small. For example, when a family or a religious community moves to a place that is not Christian, they begin to live their Christian spirituality in that new context, where they try to fit in in a friendly and kind way, and slowly begin to express it with elements of the culture they have adopted. Pastors must be willing to encourage these efforts. In this way, they form a small Christian community with new cultural characteristics. This new experience becomes a treasure for the Church, and it represents the beginning of the rise of this culture within the Church. We cannot yet speak of the evangelization of that culture, nor of its Christian transformation. But it is a good start that can easily create cross-cultural communication and a nascent evangelization of popular culture.

In this sense, it is questionable how some lay movements and religious congregations transmit their spirituality because they impose the same expressions, the same spiritual manifestations, the same style, and the same characteristics to all the peoples of the world. There, we discover what is the opposite of true inculturation, since it generates a cultural reduction of the Christian experience that is overly identified with only a partial expression. This happens when we are not able to distinguish the gospel message from its forms of expression. To concentrate excessively on certain charisms, choices, and ideas can result in a limitation of consciousness and sensitivity that makes authentic inculturation difficult and that tends to produce subtle forms of cultural subjugation, even if we try to act with extreme kindness and gentleness.

Even in Christian countries, inculturation must be deepened and enriched to avoid losing its strength and value. The pope knows that in Latin America there are Catholics who have left the Church because evangelization is lacking. There are also underworlds or subcultures in which the inculturation of the Gospel has yet to take the first steps: in the sciences, in the arts, in the business world, in politics, economics, the media, and technology. The pope never tires of reminding us of the cities of the mind and "invisible cities" (EG 74) that still need to be evangelized. The Gospel can shine a light on these places, and our spirituality is thus challenged, questioned, and enriched. In these areas, very specific cultural codes arise and develop that not everyone understands and values, except those who are already part of it because of a gift they have or because of personal choice. Those who succeed in interpreting deep human concerns will exert a great influence on a wide audience. A good movie or a television program, for example, can exert a strong influence and contribute to the emergence of trends and perspectives that will soon capture the imagination of a major portion of the population, at least for a time. We must pay special attention to these as to other cultural manifestations.

The laity forms an important part of God's people. The Second Vatican Council clearly states that the hierarchy must be at the service of the laity. Francis, if anything, goes even further: he asks the bishops not to remain before the flock but also in their midst and behind them. What, exactly, is he trying to communicate here?

To walk behind the people means to be guided by the flock, "allowing the flock to strike out on new paths" (EG 31). This is part of that confidence in the people that we discussed before. The people are a diverse network of relationships, experiences, stories, and that's where the immense wealth lies that the bishop should be able to recognize, gather together, and feed.

What roles can or should the laity take on within the Church?

Strictly speaking, they could take on all the roles that do not require the sacrament of holy orders. Only a priest can preside at the Eucharist and the sacrament of reconciliation. Only a bishop can ordain priests and deacons. But there are many things that do not require having received holy orders, many more things than we imagine. It all depends on how the Church wants to share these roles.

Let us also remember that some laypeople can have the appropriate gifts to hold positions within the church structures, but the vast majority have the gifts aimed at being a leaven for good in society. This too is serving the Church, if we consider the Church as consisting of all of us and as a community that has to reach all corners of society with the gospel proclamation and the life of Jesus.

In recent months, the Spanish newspaper El País *proposed that women should be made cardinals. Is this a viable option, in your opinion?*

In theory, yes, because the cardinalship is not a divine institution, it is a position created by the Church. There are no dogmas of faith in that regard or definitive statements, and its characteristics may change over time depending on what the Church thinks best. However, I agree with what Cardinal Rodríguez Maradiaga said in *La Repubblica* (November 22, 2013), that this could lead to a "clericalization" of women. On the other hand, a new role could be created, similar to that of the cardinals, that could function significantly in various areas of the Church.

7

New Steps Forward in Interreligious Dialogue and Ecumenism

"The Church of silence is silent no longer; it will speak through my voice," John Paul II said a few days after his election, on November 5, 1978, in Assisi. And now Pope Francis will make Wojtyla's voice his own, actualizing it in dialogue with everyone, not only with the different Christian communities and the Jewish world, but also with other religions, beginning with Islam. This could be called a sort of Ostpolitik of mercy, that of Jorge Mario Bergoglio, which aims to affect a world that has been deeply transformed by the global capitalism of the third millennium—a world in which religions, not just Islam, have a crucial role in achieving the peace "of all men of good will" whom Bergoglio addresses just as John XXIII did. "Interreligious dialogue is a priority of his ministry," as his "lieutenant" *in terra* "*infidelium*," the French cardinal of the strict Ostpolitik school, Jean-Louis Tauran, has said.

Muslims are "our brothers," and with them, Christians must cultivate "mutual respect," Francis said during the celebration of the Angelus a few days after the message was sent marking the end of Ramadan and the beginning of the feast of Eid al-Fitr. These were words of extraordinary openness and fraternity that seem to usher in a new season. But the pope has also directed similar words to the followers of other religions just as he had done, of course, for our Christian brothers. It is no coincidence that the throne of Peter is occupied in fact by the first pope who bears the name of the *Poverello* who crossed the sea to reconcile with the Sultan who had shed the blood of his brothers. It is the incarnation of the gospel of mercy that breaks down the "globalization of indifference." The new walls are not those of political-economic models like the Berlin Wall, which Wojtyla is responsible for having removed, but the barriers that do not allow civilizations to meet and live together. On this matter, for example, the prophets of the confrontation with Islam do not find a ready ear with Francis, but the "bridge builders" do, those who build up pastoral harmony among faiths, similar to what Bergoglio had already achieved in his Buenos Aires workshop. Again it was Cardinal Tauran who said, "I remember a few years ago Bergoglio had sent a priest from the diocese of Buenos Aires to Cairo to study Arabic, because he wanted someone who was capable and well trained for the dialogue with Islam. So, in this first year of his pontificate and in the current context, he has wanted to make it clear that interreligious dialogue, and in particular the dialogue with Islam, represents one of the priorities of his ministry."

Fr. Víctor, in recent decades, especially since the Second Vatican Council, we have witnessed many approaches by the Church to non-Catholics and non-Christians. In a short time, Pope Francis has brought into play several gestures in this direction, taking into account the good things that had been achieved by his predecessors. From the point of view of how he thinks and reflects on this issue, what is the new pope presenting us with?

The pope has again taken up a document of the International Theological Commission from 1996 that had been subject to much criticism. Entitled *Christianity and the World Religions,* it not only states that non-Christians can live in the grace of God, but it also recognizes the value of their rituals, their rites, and the texts of most of these religions. On this issue, Pope Francis says that "as Christians, we can also benefit from these treasures built up over many centuries, which can help us better to live our own beliefs" (EG 254). Nevertheless, it is unthinkable that we accuse him of seeking to undermine Catholic identity, because he writes that "a facile syncretism would ultimately be a totalitarian gesture on the part of those who would ignore greater values of which they are not the masters" (EG 251). In fact, he invites us to be firm in our convictions, which are a good that we can share with others. If we give up being ourselves, we will also give up the good that God has given us to share. He says it very incisively: "What is not helpful is a diplomatic openness which says 'yes' to everything in order to avoid problems, for this would be a way of deceiving others and denying them the good which we have been given to share generously with others" (EG 251). We see, then, how the pope moves wisely and in a delicate balance in dealing with this issue. In his words, there is a proper mix of openness and honesty.

———————

In the relationship with Judaism, we recall some of Cardinal Bergoglio's gestures in Buenos Aires: he often dialogued with some rabbis, so much so that one of them called him "my rabbi Bergoglio." He shared a television program with Rabbi Abraham Skorka and proposed that the Catholic University of Argentina confer upon him an honorary doctorate. What is the significance of these gestures for you?

I wish to emphasize that these were not diplomatic gestures aimed at hitting the headlines, because those same gestures caused him many problems with some nationalist anti-Semitic groups. He devoted a lot of time to these dialogues, and often did it at times and in places where no one would see him. He did it from the heart, sharing laughter and tears with his audience. I would, however, dwell on the honorary doctorate that he wanted to give Rabbi Skorka, because as rector of the Catholic University, I played an active part in it. It was a gesture that surpassed any form of courtesy or diplomacy, since it implied a recognition of the wisdom and wealth of knowledge and doctrine of this Jewish teacher that could also benefit us Catholics. This event did finally cause the ultraconservative groups to lose patience. At that time, they took it out on Bergoglio especially (and also on me). You can still read their infuriated speeches on some websites.

In addition to those steps and others carried out by the pope, what innovations does Evangelii Gaudium *usher in, what new ideas?*

There are various things that attract much attention. One of these is that he grieves not only for the persecutions perpetrated against the Jews, but also, and especially, for those in which he still sees Christians involved, not only by their actions—which are less frequent—but more often "by silence." This sentence is also very interesting: "Dialogue and friendship with the children of Israel are part of the life of Jesus' disciples" (EG 248). It is not an activity and neither is it a task of convenience, but this friendship is an integral part of our lives!

What is even more meaningful from the theological point of view is this statement that is absolutely new to the magisterium and that invites us to take a step forward in the reflection and action of the Church, according to which "God continues to work among the people of the Old Covenant and to bring forth treasures of wisdom which flow from their encounter with his word. For this reason, the Church is also enriched when she receives the values of Judaism" (EG 249). All this is very powerful because it is easy to accept that Christians should receive the wealth contained in the Old Testament, including the contributions of Judaism prior to Jesus Christ.

However, here it is referring to current values, concerning what God "continues to work" today through them. They do not need to become converts, and the Jewish religion does not need to disappear, because it surely has a value in the eyes of the supernatural God. The same thing that Bergoglio said when he conferred an honorary doctorate on a rabbi is today repeated with magisterial words, when they refer to the "treasures of wisdom" that spring from the encounter of Jews with the divine Word. I hope that this step forward, which is encapsulated in a short paragraph, is carefully taken into account by theologians who study the relationship of Christians to Judaism and by those who are engaged in these relations within the Holy See.

On the other hand, Pope Francis refers back to a request by Cardinal Walter Kasper, who claimed that the Jews were not supposed to be part of the missionary plans that included the "conversion" of others, since the biblical meaning of conversion cannot be applied in their case. The pope endorses this reflection when he says that we Christians must not include Jews "among those called to turn from idols and to serve the true God" (cf. 1 Thess 1:9). With them, we believe in the one God who acts in history, and with them, we accept his revealed word.

Does the pope also speak about the difficulties that evangelization has met and still meets in Islamic countries?

There is a paragraph of admirable delicacy and tenderness in which the pope is able to touch on an issue that is thorny and painful. Francis is capable of expressing reproach and recrimination that otherwise would seem aggressive or ideological in character in a way that leads us to listen to him with respect and attention. First, he says, "Faced with disconcerting episodes of violent fundamentalism, our respect for true followers of Islam should lead us to avoid hateful generalizations" (EG 253). Deploring fundamentalism "on both sides" (EG 250), he states that "we

Christians should embrace with affection and respect Muslim immigrants to our countries" (EG 253). These are statements that call us to have true and sincere dialogue with Muslims.

To these gestures of openness and understanding, the pope dares to add, "We Christians should embrace with affection and respect Muslim immigrants to our countries in the same way that we hope and ask to be received and respected in countries of Islamic tradition" (EG 253). There is no need to recall the tremendous difficulties faced by Christians in Saudi Arabia to keep their faith alive, or the violent persecutions or murders in Pakistan, Indonesia, and other countries. But Francis addresses himself primarily to the authorities of those countries, to ask them with magnificent and indisputable simplicity, "I ask and I humbly entreat those countries to grant Christians freedom to worship and to practice their faith, in light of the freedom which followers of Islam enjoy in Western countries!" (EG 253). What can you say when faced with words like these? He did not want to claim full freedom for the missionary task, but he touches upon it in this paragraph. If we at least begin to listen, we could open the door to major changes, which, in any case, will require many years.

Ecumenical dialogue is always a work in progress in Rome. And it is very dear to those who guide the Church. Benedict XVI explicitly stated that unity among Christians was the plan for his pontificate. What proposals has Francis set in motion and does he intend to set in motion regarding this issue?

There is only one important paragraph exclusively dedicated to ecumenism itself. It has the advantage of summarizing in a few words the most beautiful things that John Paul II taught us in his encyclical *Ut Unum Sint*—for example, that there are many things that unite us and that we can learn from each other.

However, the most interesting part of this paragraph is its reference to the mission *ad gentes*, from which one senses that the pope is deeply concerned about the scandal of divisions in mission countries. What is very striking is his assertion that "the immense numbers of people who have not received the Gospel of Jesus Christ cannot leave us indifferent. Consequently, commitment to a unity which helps them to accept Jesus Christ can no longer be a matter of mere diplomacy or forced compliance, but rather an indispensable path to evangelization" (EG 246). This encourages missionaries not to worry so much about Catholic identity or not to be obsessed with the absolute purity of Catholicism in competition with other Christian denominations. Instead, it suggests that we aspire to what is more important, which is that non-Christians come to encounter Jesus Christ, and that we downplay the things that separate us from non-Catholics, so that we can carry on the work of evangelization united. Yes, together! He says very clearly, "If we concentrate on the convictions we share, and if we keep in mind the principle of the hierarchy of truths, we will be able to progress speedily toward common expressions of proclamation, service and witness" (EG 246). This is a very important contribution to ecumenism and mission.

Compared to the ongoing challenge of religious freedom—which is not a secondary topic in the texts of the Second Vatican Council— what new approach does the pope bring?

In addition to the call to religious freedom in Muslim countries, there is another aspect that should be exposed courageously, namely, those extreme forms of secularism that presume to privatize religions by reducing them "to the quiet obscurity of the individual's conscience or to relegate them to the enclosed precincts of churches, synagogues or mosques." The pope does not consider this secularism "a healthy pluralism" but rather "a new form of discrimination and authoritarianism" that "feed resentment rather than tolerance and peace" (EG 255). True to his powerful social commitment, he argues that "it is no longer possible to claim that religion should be restricted to the private sphere and that it exists only to prepare souls for heaven. We know that God wants his children to be happy in this world too" (EG 182). As a result, "No one can demand that religion should be relegated to the inner sanctum of personal life, without influence on societal and national life, without concern for the soundness of civil institutions, without a right to offer an opinion on events affecting society" (EG 183).

Faced with this trend present in some western countries and their prejudices against the contribution of religions to public debate, the pope also uses a reflection taken from North American theology. This is where in all areas, both in the public and academic spheres, he asks for a reinstatement of the classical religious texts, which are despised "due to the myopia of a certain rationalism. Is it reasonable and enlightened to dismiss certain writings simply because they arose in a context of religious belief? These writings include principles which are profoundly humanistic and, albeit tinged with religious symbols and teachings, they have a certain value for reason" (EG 256). This is one of the issues in which the depth and courage of Pope Francis's thoughts emerge most effectively.

8

The Church, Politics, and the Economy

*E*vangelii Gaudium is not a social encyclical and, therefore, does not develop a broad discussion on the always delicate issues contained in the Church's social doctrine: humanity, work, and the state. Yet, *Evangelii Gaudium* does devote a large part of its reflection to these issues and it does so in a sharp and somewhat surprising way, especially where Pope Francis reaffirms "the intimate connection between evangelization and human development" (EG 178) and the right of bishops "to issue opinions on everything related to people's lives" (no. 182). "No one," the pope writes, "can demand that religion should be relegated to the inner sanctum of personal life, without influence on societal and national life" (no. 183). Here we also find the option for the poor, who "have much to teach us," the invitation to take care of the weakest: the homeless, drug addicts, refugees, indigenous peoples, the elderly who are alone and abandoned, migrants, victims of trafficking, and unborn children, who are "the most defenseless and innocent of all, who today are being denied human dignity" (no. 213) ("we should not expect," writes the pope, "that the Church will change its position on these issues: it is not progressive to endeavor to solve problems by eliminating a human life" [no. 214]). There is a focus on peace and dialogue and cooperation "with all political, social, religious and cultural realities." "In our dealings with the world," he concludes, "we are told to give reasons for our hope, but not as an enemy who critiques and condemns....Only the person who feels happiness in seeking the good of others, in desiring their happiness, can be a missionary" (nos. 271, 272).

How does the pope present the social dimension of evangelization?

Although the central theme of *Evangelii Gaudium* is the "'proclamation" of the Gospel, the pope did not want its social dimension to be left out, or to make it seem a secondary aspect or one that could be ignored. Thus, he dwells on the socially inescapable content of the kerygma that constitutes its essence. Community life and commitment to others can be found at the heart of the Gospel. However, he strongly suggests that we not make ourselves addicted to this message, that we not convert it into obvious and repetitive words, but that we make it take flesh in us: "How dangerous and harmful this is, for it makes us lose our amazement, our excitement and our zeal for living the Gospel of fraternity and justice!" (EG 179).

According to Pope Francis, it is not possible to reduce the Christian life to a personal relationship with the Lord. Reading the scriptures, it is clear that the proposal of the Gospel is the kingdom of God: "Strive first for the kingdom of God and his righteousness" (Matt 6:33). We must love God who wants to rule over the world, and "to the extent that he reigns within us, the life of society will be a setting for universal fraternity, justice, peace and dignity. Both Christian preaching and life, then, are meant to have an impact on society" (EG 180). This phrase reminds us that evangelization must take care "of each man and of the whole man" (*Populorum Progressio* 14).

It is interesting to see how, despite the fact that the Church's teaching spans various subjects, the pope wants to emphasize the two that he feels are the most important for the future of humanity: social peace and the inclusion of the poor in society.

Some continue to state that the option for the poor is a sociological issue that politicizes the Gospel. This seems to be the case with this pope's approach. Why?

Because from our faith in Christ who became poor, and was always close to the poor, comes the concern for the integral development of those most left to themselves, those who "are discarded and thrown away." The pope insists on the word *solidarity*, because "these convictions and habits of solidarity, when they are put into practice, open the way to other structural transformations and make them possible. Changing structures without generating new convictions and attitudes will only ensure that those same structures will become, sooner or later, corrupt, oppressive and ineffectual" (EG 189). Obviously, Francis is also concerned to expose the structural causes of poverty. He is critical of trickle-down theories, the absolute authority of the markets and financial speculation, and he lays bare the roots of inequality. More than anything, though, he wants all of us, rather than talking too much, to take up our responsibilities for making sure that others can live with greater dignity.

The call to solidarity with the poor pervades the whole Bible and the teaching of the Church. It is the pure Gospel, and it cannot and should not be diluted. The pope reminds us that chapter 14 of Luke's Gospel offers a powerful teaching: it says that when you hold a banquet, you should not invite either friends or rich neighbors but, above all, the poor and the sick, those who are usually despised and forgotten, those who "cannot repay you" (Luke 14:14). He dwells at length on this and even speaks of the cry of the poor and the oppressed, which occurs so frequently in the Bible and among liberation theologians.

The pope cites St. Paul especially when he came to the apostles in Jerusalem to ensure that he "was not running, or had not run, in vain" (Gal 2:2), and the only criterion of authenticity that they imposed was that he "remember the poor" (2:10).

This great yardstick, which ensured that the Pauline communities did not allow themselves to be devoured by the individualistic lifestyle of the pagans, has considerable relevance in the present context, where a new individualistic paganism tends to develop. The beauty of the Gospel cannot always be adequately clear to us, but there is one sign that should never be missing: the option for those who are last, for those whom society rejects and throws away. Therefore, whether we like it or not, we absolutely need a Church that is poor and for the poor and "this message is so clear and direct, so simple and eloquent, that no ecclesial interpretation has the right to relativize it" (EG 194). Of course, when one reads the biblical texts that the pope mentions, it is very unlikely that this message could come out weakened.

All this, rather than being political, is a matter of deep faith. From a pragmatic point of view, it will always seem a better choice to devote oneself to the dominant classes of society, to those who hold power. In the current model of personal gain, it seems to make no sense to invest in those who are left behind, the weak or less gifted, so that they can make their way in life. The option for the poor breaks this pragmatism and becomes a matter of faith. One thing I did not understand, however, was the senior representative of the Vatican who told some nuns who lived in a poor neighborhood that there was no future for them there.

The pope's emphasis is not ideological, it is evangelical.

However, when Jesus spoke, some left because they could not bear to listen to him. He upsets our habits and our comforts. Francis's visit to Lampedusa—at the periphery of Europe—with its enormous symbolic power was extremely disturbing to some, because it forced them to face a drama that everyone had always tried to hide. This pope, however, will never allow us to forget the poor, and he will always find a way to remind us that they are here, in our world. Christians who feel annoyed by this social discourse are obliged to listen to the cry of the poor and of poor countries, since "the need to heed this plea is itself born of the liberating action of grace within each of us, and thus it is not a question of a mission reserved only to a few" (EG 188).

Why in the context of the call to poverty, and not elsewhere, does he state his firm opposition to abortion?

Because he wants it to be an important contribution to the public debate, since "this defense of unborn life is closely linked to the defense of each and every other human right. It involves the conviction that a human being is always sacred and inviolable….Once this conviction disappears, so do solid and lasting foundations for the defense of human rights, which would always be subject to the passing whims of the powers that be….It is not 'progressive' to try to resolve problems by eliminating a human life" (EG 213–14). By saying this, he reveals the inconsistency of abortion in a political project that claims to respect the dignity and rights of every human without exception. I believe that the pope hits the nail on the head by highlighting this inconsistency within the rhetoric of some progressive groups.

What is the pope's proposal for social peace?

The topic of social harmony and the culture of encounter is the second of the pope's strong emphases in relation to social teaching. It's a tough but much needed message requiring a lot of effort in the reconstruction of the social fabric, since Francis is convinced that all wars are futile. From this arises, for example, his strong opposition to military intervention in Syria. It is a journey of sacrifice, of dialogue and negotiations, that eventually becomes an "exchange of gifts" (EG 246).

The pope, however, would never advocate social peace at the expense of silencing our defense of the poor and what we have to say in the face of injustice. It would be like allowing "the more affluent to placidly support their lifestyle while others have to make do as they can" (EG 218). This is not acceptable, since the "demands involving the distribution of wealth, concern for the poor and human rights cannot be suppressed under the guise of creating a consensus on paper or a transient peace for a contented minority. The dignity of the human person and the common good rank higher than the comfort of those who refuse to renounce their privileges" (no. 218). The pope knows that, if peace does not arise from the integral development of all, it will always sow the seed of new conflicts and various forms of violence. When we read these paragraphs, we seem to be listening again to the prophetic denunciations of Isaiah or St. John Chrysostom.

The road to social peace is a long road of healing wounds, dialogue, and meetings that contribute to creating a "culture of encounter" (EG 220). We Christians cannot remain on the theoretical level or simply denounce the errors of others. If we are truly interested in building peace, then we should feel obliged to set an example with ecumenical and interreligious dialogue. I believe that this is the only way we can understand Bergoglio's great dedication to dialogue with non-Catholics. If we are not able to talk, meet, and understand those who are not Catholic, then we can never achieve the effort of dialogue and understanding needed from politics.

When he refers to building social peace, Francis, as already mentioned, proposes four principles: "time is greater than space," "unity prevails over conflict," "realities are more important than ideas," and, "the whole is greater than the part." Are these principles useful only for the purposes of politics, or can we all benefit from them?

To make progress in the building of any community, Bergoglio has always argued, even from the time when he was a cardinal, that there were four principles related to bipolar tensions inherent in any social reality that specifically guide the development of social life and the building of a people. However, it is very interesting that in *Evangelii Gaudium*, he does not present them as a social teaching only, but also shows how they should be implemented in a pastoral setting. In other words, they are not only valid for a president or a ruler, but also for a pastor and any leader of a community. Therefore, they serve as a pastoral examination of conscience or as a yardstick against which can be measured the entire strategy of any leader, the whole pastoral plan and the exercise of any ministry within the Church.

For example, the pope teaches us that time is greater than space. In this way, he invites us to work for the long haul without being obsessed with immediate results. He teaches us that we must not give preference to space, that is, the dominion of power, so much as to the timing of a plan. On the other hand, sometimes we can go crazy trying to fix everything in the here and now. This also applies to a mother, when it is said that she should not be obsessed with controlling everything her children do, but should concern herself with helping them develop processes for growth. These processes will cause them to mature and will protect them more than any external control can. At the same time, however, Pope Francis says, "This criterion also applies to evangelization, which calls for attention to the bigger picture, openness to suitable processes and concern for the long run....the enemy can intrude upon the kingdom and sow harm, but ultimately he is defeated by the goodness of the wheat" (EG 225).

The other principles too can be useful for everyone because they teach us to develop a communion even among our differences, to resolve conflicts at a higher level that creates a new synthesis, to prevent our conceptual ideas from alienating us from reality, to build many-sided strategies that combine the best aspects of one and all. These attitudes that the pope is proposing with his four principles allow us to take appropriate action in all communities and in all human relationships, and lead us to be fruitful, to produce new activities, and to sow good in society.

Popes have always made important contributions to world politics and international relations. Fr. Víctor, how, in your opinion, is Pope Francis also contributing to these two important areas?

Here is a valuable fact: when he presents himself as a pope from "the ends of the earth," Francis does not use the phrase in a derogatory way, because for him it is not a limitation but an asset. Observing reality from the ends of the earth helps to provide new perspectives with the positive meaning of "pre-judice," as the philosopher Hans-Georg Gadamer taught. In fact, on May 26, 2013, the pope said that "reality is better understood from the periphery, not from the center." That's a very bold phrase and it has powerful political content.

Furthermore, the very composition of the population of Argentina, full of immigrants from across the globe, has caused the country itself to become a land of encounter. Therefore, in his first act with the diplomatic corps assigned to the Holy See, Francis said, "My own origins push me to work to build bridges." I think the pope looks with faith to his origins and is convinced that he was elected to bring new horizons to the universal Church and through it to the whole world—a vision that those at the center of the world could not distinguish clearly.

We have to acknowledge that his initiatives are producing many results. The Iranian president, Hassan Rohani, listens respectfully to what this pope says and has posted on his Twitter account that "today more than ever, Islam and Christianity are in need of dialogue, as the basic conflict between religions is more than anything else ignorance and lack of mutual understanding." He added that, according to the doctrine of their respective religions, the Vatican and Iran have "common enemies," such as terrorism and extremism, and "similar goals," such as overcoming injustice and poverty in the world.

Some politicians grumble, "Why doesn't this man calm down and leave us alone?" This is understandable when you read some of the pope's harsh words: "I ask God to give us more politicians capable of sincere and effective dialogue aimed at healing the deepest roots—and not simply the appearances—of the evils in our world!...I beg the Lord to grant us more politicians who are genuinely disturbed by the state of society, the people, the lives of the poor! It is vital that government leaders and financial leaders take heed and broaden their horizons" (EG 205). Also, "Sometimes I wonder if there are people in today's world who are really concerned about generating processes of people-building, as opposed to obtaining immediate results which yield easy, quick short-term political gains, but do not enhance human fullness. History will perhaps judge the latter" (EG 224).

I believe that we should not expect Pope Francis to maintain a low profile in the Church's participation in the public and political spheres. In fact, shortly after he was elected pope, he said, "I hope that this is also an opportunity to embark on a journey with those few countries that still do not have diplomatic relations with the Holy See." In one year, he received nearly thirty heads of state and government, as well as numerous leaders of several international bodies. In addition, on November 14, 2013, he visited the Quirinal Palace and will certainly take other initiatives similar to his attempt to prevent the spread of the conflict in Syria (let us pray to God that he remains in good health). These initiatives will be mainly related to two major social issues that most concern him: social peace and the inclusion of the poor in society. For this reason, when he had to decide which theme to propose to the Pontifical Academies of Sciences and Social Sciences for their research, he had no doubts and asked them to dedicate themselves to the issue of human trafficking as a form of modern slavery, because he wants them to provide a solid contribution to this subject. I did hear that a member of these Academies was a little angry and commented that this matter is of little importance for academic research.

We must not delude ourselves. Unfortunately, some intellectual circles, especially the more conservative ones, spend their time focusing on any details that they find useful for ridiculing the pope. They say, "Why has he used this word? Why did he not say that? Why did he not explain these things? Why is he not more specific?" I believe that they cannot see the wood for the trees. However, Pope Francis does not speak or act hastily or impulsively. His gestures, his actions, and his sentences always have a long-term goal to which he has given much thought and that he has well thought out. Because of this, while others content themselves with discussing at a superficial level and thereby risk wasting their energies, he goes firmly ahead, free from concern for appearance and with resolute patience. Let's not forget that the value of something is also recognized by the effects it produces.

It is no secret to anyone that in Evangelii Gaudium, *the sections that the pope devoted to the economy have caused quite an uproar, especially among neoliberal economists who have criticized him harshly. How do you explain their annoyance, and how would he respond to them?*

The problem is that many have only focused on some of the harshest expressions and taken them out of context. In order to understand what the pope has to say on the economy, we have to read all of the text in which he lays out his position, or at least chapters 2 and 4 in their entirety. After you have read everything, you will understand that the pope's position is actually very balanced.

On the one hand, he highly values business when he says that "business is a vocation, and a noble vocation," especially for "striving to increase the goods of this world and to make them more accessible to all" (EG 203). On the other hand, and this is the most important aspect, his words about the economy should be read together with his statements on the need for science to contribute to the teaching of the Church (nos. 40, 133, 182) with its specific methodology and legitimate autonomy (no. 243). This also applies to the economy. Consistently, the pope acknowledges that he does not have to "offer a detailed and comprehensive analysis of contemporary reality" (no. 51) and that he does not "have a monopoly on the interpretation of social realities or the proposal of solutions to contemporary problems" (no. 184).

I think that this constitutes a very important context right now for expressing one's opinion freely on issues related to the economy or other social sciences, but without denying the pope's words their exhortative tone. The economic reality and the solution to the problems of today's world require scientific analysis that might even contradict some of the pope's claims on these issues, which are, after all, not dogmas of faith.

But he does not want to keep quiet about the troubling problems of the poorest countries, which will not be solved only hoping for a spontaneous worldwide trickle-down effect as a result of the growth of other nations. The pope thinks this kind of thinking is naïve. What are required are generous interventions and actions of solidarity by developed countries in order to help overcome poverty in the poorest countries, because "the mere fact that some people are born in places with fewer resources or less development does not justify the fact that they are living with less dignity" (EG 190). It is therefore clear that if "everything comes under the laws of competition and the survival of the fittest" (no. 53), there will be no way out for them. For this reason, he calls us to "hear the plea of other peoples and other regions" (no. 190), just as he deplores that "the current model, with its emphasis on success and self-reliance, does not appear to favor an investment in efforts to help the slow, the weak or the less talented to find opportunities in life" (no. 209).

Nor has he denied that, in some places on the planet, in recent decades, poverty has decreased. What he says instead is that, globally, inequality is increasing because the speed and intensity of growth of those who are better off is not at the same pace as those who are less fortunate and are more and more distant "from the prosperity enjoyed by those happy few" (EG 56). I am aware that some economists distort the pope's words to make him appear naïve or misinformed. It is a controversy reminiscent of those who say that the pope will not let them speak against abortion, when in fact what he asks them to do is something very specific: not to speak "always" and "only" about those issues.

Let us consider well the terms that the pope uses. What he has twice refuted is the "absolute" autonomy of the marketplace (EG 56, 202). Who can contradict this? He says in a balanced way that "growth in justice requires more than economic growth, while presupposing such growth" (EG 204). It requires action by the state, but he adds that "welfare projects, which meet certain urgent needs, should be considered merely temporary responses" (EG 202), and "I am far from proposing an irresponsible populism" (EG 204). It is perhaps better if we read it in its entirety without allowing our emotions to obscure our view. Perhaps the pope will also make a contribution to economists, provided that they do not want to take on an infallibility that the pope prefers not to flaunt.

9

Fr. Jorge:
A Personal Memoir

Jorge Mario Bergoglio is the first pope to come out of the Americas; he had been archbishop of Buenos Aires since 1998. He is a leading figure in the whole continent and a simple pastor who has been much loved in his diocese and who has traveled far and wide, including on the subway and buses. "My people are poor and I'm one of them," he once said, explaining his choice to live in an apartment and prepare his own dinner alone. He has always recommended mercy, courage, and an open-door policy to his priests. The worst thing that can happen in the Church, he has explained in various circumstances, "is what Henri de Lubac called spiritual worldliness," which means "putting oneself at the center." And when he refers to social justice, he invites us to take up the catechism, the Ten Commandments, and the Beatitudes. The biography published on the Vatican's official website states that "despite his reserved character, Bergoglio has become a landmark for the position he took during the economic crisis that shook the country in 2001."

He was born on December 17, 1936, in the Argentine capital, the son of immigrants from Piedmont: his father, Mario, was an accountant employed by the railroad, while his mother, Regina Sivori, took care of the house and the education of their five children. He graduated as a chemical engineer and then chose the path of the priesthood by entering the diocesan seminary. On March 11, 1958, he proceeded to the novitiate in the Society of Jesus. He completed his studies in humanities in Chile, and in 1963, he returned to Argentina and graduated in philosophy at the Colegio Máximo de San José in San Miguel. Between 1964 and 1965, he was professor of literature and psychology at the College of the Immaculate Conception in Santa Fe, and in 1966, he taught the same subjects at the Colegio del Salvador in Buenos Aires. From 1967 to 1970, he studied theology and graduated, again from the Colegio Máximo de San José.

On December 13, 1969, he was ordained a priest. He continued his preparation in Spain between 1970 and 1971, and on April 22, 1973, he made his final profession in the Jesuits. Back in Argentina, he became novice master at Villa Barilari in San Miguel, a professor in the theology faculty, an adviser in the province of the Society of Jesus, and the rector of the college.

On July 31, 1973, he was elected provincial of the Jesuits in Argentina. Six years later, he resumed his academic work and, between 1980 and 1986, was the new rector of Colegio Máximo de San José as well as a parish priest again in San Miguel. In March 1986, he went to Germany to complete his doctoral thesis on Romano Guardini, but the project was not completed. His superiors sent him to the Colegio del Salvador in Buenos Aires and then to the Jesuit community in the city of Cordoba as spiritual director and confessor.

He became a close associate of Cardinal Quarracino in Buenos Aires. On May 20, 1992, John Paul II appointed him Titular Bishop of Auca and Auxiliary Bishop of Buenos Aires. On June 27 in the cathedral, he received his episcopal ordination from the cardinal. He chose *Miserando atque eligendo* ("By showing compassion and by choosing") as his motto and included on his emblem the Christogram IHS, symbol of the Society of Jesus. He was immediately appointed episcopal vicar of the Flores area, and on December 21, 1993, he became vicar general. So it was no surprise when he was promoted to Coadjutor Archbishop of Buenos Aires on June 3, 1997. No more than nine months later, on February 28,

1998, on the death of Cardinal Antonio Quarracino, he succeeded him as archbishop, primate of Argentina, Ordinary for the faithful of the Eastern rite who were resident in the country, and Great Chancellor of the Catholic University.

In the consistory of February 21, 2001, John Paul II created him cardinal priest of St. Robert Bellarmine. In October 2001, he was appointed General Relator to the tenth Ordinary General Assembly of the Synod of Bishops, on the episcopal ministry. Meanwhile, in Latin America, his popularity increased. In 2002, he declined the appointment as president of the Episcopal Conference of Argentina, but three years later, he was elected and then reelected for another three years in 2008. Meanwhile, in April 2005, he participated in the conclave that elected Pope Benedict XVI.

As archbishop of Buenos Aires, which has three million people, he initiated a missionary project focused on communion and evangelization. It had four main objectives: open and brotherly communities; an informed laity, playing a lead role; evangelization efforts addressed to every inhabitant of the city; and assistance to the poor and the sick. He invited priests and laypeople to work together.

In September 2009, he launched a nationwide campaign of solidarity for the bicentennial of the country's independence: two hundred works of charity to be achieved by 2016. And, on a continental level, he had high hopes for the message of the Aparecida Conference in 2007, so much so that he defined it as "the *Evangelii Nuntiandi* of Latin America."

Fr. Víctor, there are few like you who have had the opportunity to meet frequently with Cardinal Bergoglio. When and where did you meet, and what moments do you remember most?

I met him for the first time at the Faculty of Theology of Buenos Aires when I was just a professor, and we talked for about two minutes about Pablo Tissera, a very generous Jesuit priest who had been my spiritual director. However, he knew of me through the comments of people who had read my little books on spirituality. Usually, I spoke with him for only a few minutes, even when I was rector of his university. When I had doubts about something, I sent him an email, and shortly afterward, he would call me with an answer.

Here, I can only cite three special moments in which we chatted for a longer amount of time: one was in 2007, after we had come back from the Fifth Conference of Bishops in Apare-cida, where I represented the priests of Argentina. I was traveling with him on the flight back to Buenos Aires, and for three hours, we discussed some issues that have helped me to understand his thinking. Another important moment took place in his office. Some anonymous people sent critical comments to the Vatican on three of my articles. After a year and a half, the answers that I had sent to clarify my thinking did not seem to convince my recipients. On that occasion, we had a great spiritual conversation, in which he told me to keep my head up and not allow them to take away my dignity. Finally, my meeting with him in St. Martha's in the month of August 2013, when I embraced him, after having already received my episcopal ordination.

You are a priest. Which of Bergoglio's teachings has been most useful for you in your experience as a priest?

Although we have a great affinity of ideas, for me, he was and above all is a great father figure who has been able to recognize and promote the best in me. In this way, with tenderness, he has put up with my mistakes, my vanity, and my impatience, and always encouraged me, especially through his witness, to continue to mature and grow. That is for me his most important teaching, because it has allowed me to understand how priests should treat people.

Before the last conclave, had you ever imagined that Cardinal Bergoglio could be elected? What did you think when he appeared at the central loggia of the Vatican Basilica on March 13, 2013?

He has not changed much. What is new is his great joy and very special strength, given his age. But he has always been very close to the people, especially to the poor and the simple. He was never a "prince," and that has not changed. However, even when he was archbishop, he was slowly retreating and preferred not to appear much in public. In addition, there were too many persecution campaigns orchestrated by some very conservative groups within the Church, and I believe that worried him greatly. Today, now that he is pope, with the new gift that the Holy Spirit has bestowed upon him, he has abandoned those fears and allowed his best side to emerge. This has renewed his enthusiasm and his energy.

Dear Fr. Víctor, to conclude, what gesture or words from Cardinal Bergoglio in Buenos Aires remain indelibly in your memory?

A gesture: during a meeting with evangelical communities when he knelt down and asked them to pray for him. Among his words: those I have just mentioned, when he told me during a very difficult time, "Keep your head up and do not let them take away your dignity."